# Contents

To my dear hard-working, non-conformist mother without whom, if there is a success-story in these pages, nothing would have been possible.

# Acknowledgments

I should like to express my indebtedness in the production of this book to Messrs. Wilson Elstubb, Bagenal Harvey, Alan Ross, and the staff of Bective School, Northampton; to my wife Ursula; and in particular to Mr. John Arlott who has turned the arid plain of my indolence into a productive garden.

# Preface

My aim is not to tell merely what I have done in the game, but also what the game has done for me. My book is an expression of thanks for many hours of physical and mental enjoyment, to say nothing of material rewards. Players come and go; performance succeeds performance: yet the game remains, and will, I hope, for many years to come. The fast bowler, perhaps more than anyone else, is aware of the transience of the individual and the permanence of the sport. I hope that the opinions expressed in this book will do something to ensure the continuance of what many people think is a dying game.

Nowadays the fashion in cricket-writing is towards the salacious jargon of the gossip column, the salty taste of betrayed boudoir secrets. There are two unfortunate aspects of these revelations of dressing-room confidences. One regrettably, is that the facts are too often right; the other is that cricket gives full scope to the expression of the good and bad side of every player's personality, and so it is easy to seek out weaknesses of character, or flaws of behaviour and set them down in print. Very few people would follow cricket if there were not colourful players who really let themselves go on the field. Cricket followers are just as interested in what Freddie Trueman said to the umpire at Leeds in 1955 as politicians and historians are in what Gladstone said on Home Rule in 1885. It is right that it should be so. It is the personalities in the game who make it colourful, and I sincerely hope that we shall not lose them.

Any cricket book worth its salt therefore must give preferential treatment to the individual traits of the players who are its main characters. For my part, I shall not deal in dirt, but should there be any occasion to take any individual or body of individuals to task, I shall exercise every man's prerogative of objective criticism, in a way, I hope, which will serve the best interests of the game. In that context the failure of touring sides must inevitably lead to blame being heaped upon the heads of those responsible. It is right that it should be so. The M.C.C. are right to prevent the betrayal of dressing-room confidences, but they cannot, even should they want to, stifle justifiable criticism.

Do not take this book down from the shelf with the idea that it is just another cricket book. Many volumes have been written on the game: some good, many excellent, and just as many bad. In content, mine may be ordinary; in expression and style, less than significant; but it is the sincere, personal work of someone who is trying to say thank-you for all the pleasure which cricket has given to him.

F. T.

NORTHAMPTON
September 1960

CHAPTER ONE

# Fast Bowling is a Feeling

'*Be not afraid of greatness: some men are born great, some achieve greatness and some have greatness thrust upon them.*' It seems the fashion nowadays to have someone else to write one's cricket autobiography. I admit openly that Shakespeare 'ghosted' my opening sentence, but my indebtedness to any ghost ends there, for mine is a personal message which I want to deliver myself.

It is hard to shake the habit of quotation and, moreover, I was taught that a dictum is an appropriate way to begin any literary effort. More than that, the quotation is quite apposite since it seems to me, looking back, that greatness *was*, indeed, thrust upon me. One night I went to sleep an ordinary fast bowler who enjoyed playing cricket, only to wake up the next day dubbed a violent hurricane, frequenting the coasts of China and Japan – a Typhoon. For a while I hated the nickname with which the Press had labelled me. Even my team mates began calling me the famous oriental fast bowler – and I resented being a Typhoon to the world at large; the geography was wrong. At first I chafed under the name, but then I accepted it and, in the years of declining pace, I was finally glad of the consolation of the title.

It is not now as it was of yore, for my days of success are past: and even those golden years were far removed from my youth and childhood. When I was young my whole being revolved around cricket and the delight of fast bowling. No matter what the surroundings, my only concern was cricket. It was second nature for me to break into a run down school corridors and, in imagination, bowl out Bradman with an unplayable break-back. The day was not long enough for me and close of play came too soon. Each night I went to sleep, fists clenched, and the prayer on my lips, 'Please God, let me do well at cricket. Let me play for England.'

For my life I cannot remember when I did not bowl fast. More than that, I cannot recollect when I ever gave second thoughts to any bowling less than the quickest I could possibly attain. I have always put my all into bowling: my body, my heart and my soul. I never thought to do otherwise. In my later cricket years, I often relaxed at the nets. Yet even when I was fooling about, trying to bowl spinners, I always bowled about twice as fast as I should have done. No wonder I could never spin the ball.

Fast bowling was just second nature to me. It was as simple as that. There was no need for self-analysis, it was just something I did, and that was that. I never gave a second thought to the whys and wherefores – not, that is, until a few years later.

It was in Adelaide that I first began to wonder *why* I bowled fast. The evening was stiflingly hot, though the day had been even hotter, as I can well vouch, for I had been fielding all day in the Test Match. Still, I did not mind the heat, for on that day of days in 1955 we had just won the Ashes in Australia for the first time in 25 years. I was sitting in the lounge of a house on Mount Lofty, just outside the city, and beneath our windows the coloured lights of the highways, orange and blue, homed on the town centre like so many streams of tracers. My companions and I were drinking coffee, waiting, like the rest of the world on that torrid night, for the relief of the cool night breeze.

We were a mixed bunch, to say the least. If an inventory were made, it would have included a painter, a poet and – no, not fiddler and buffoon – but a cricketer and broadcaster. It was the painter who really intrigued me. He was French, and was dressed in a most Gallic and picturesque way. His clothes were almost like those of a French légionnaire, for he had the same baggy pantaloons. In a way I envied him, for I should have thought he was cool, and I certainly was not. The conversation turned, as it was bound to do with three cricket enthusiasts in the room, to the game in general and to my own department of fast bowling in particular. You will notice that I said there were only three enthusiasts. The Frenchman could not understand cricket. We accept this, I think, as a national characteristic. More than any other part of the game, however, he was horrified by fast bowling, which he regarded as brutal. I suppose that, in a way, he was right, for fast bowling does involve a high proportion of brute physical force. It must seem a little unjust and more than a little dangerous at times that big men are allowed to hurl hard leather balls at inoffensive batsmen. Monsieur attributed sinister motives to people who indulged in this pastime. If I can recollect his phraseology, he seemed to be under the impression that I was suffering from an inverted Oedipus complex. Not having gone to one of the greater universities, this took me some little time to work out. Eventually I gathered that he thought that some parental hatred had made me sour towards the whole human race, and this was the reason why I took my revenge on innocent batsmen. Was it so ridiculous? I wondered. The thought began a train of ideas and, from the ruck of reflections, one stood out above all others: cricket is a game: fast bowling is for me the best part of that game and its motivating force is not hatred of the batsman but purely the enjoyment and the satisfaction of bowling fast. A little hatred helps though!

Lord Byron once coined the thought 'High mountains are a feeling'. Had I not known his background, I should have suspected Byron of being a fast bowler, for how closely it mirrors my own sentiments about bowling fast! Truly fast bowling carries with it a sensation of pleasure; it is to be borne along in a sense of elation. There is the approach to the marker which measures the length of the run. I wonder if my run is long enough; or is it too long? A feeling of uncertainty scars the ground with a little shuffle and then away, long and loping, counting mechanically yet rhythmically the nine strides of my approach. My body bows, head forward, preparing to rise, reaching, clawing for height before bringing the ball banging down at the batsman. I feel my legs tense, my head is on one side and the wickets are in my sights. There is a sudden shock, shaking me to the skull, as the stiff left leg crashes into unsympathetic turf, and my whole body flings itself after the ball, as if in malediction towards the batsman. The batsman seems to be stooping in an effort to pick up the flight of the ball earlier. Or could it be that he is cowering slightly, anticipating the ball, fearful of its speed and doubtful about my intentions? There is the breathless moment of the batsman's quicksilver duck;

the moment of truth as the ball finds the edge of the bat, and the slips snatch their prey off the very ground.

To bowl quick is to revel in the glad animal action; to thrill in physical prowess and to enjoy a certain sneaking feeling of superiority over the other mortals who play the game. No batsman likes quick bowling, and this knowledge gives one a sense of omnipotence.

Kortright, the famous Essex fast bowler of old, said that he never swung the ball. Apparently he had no need to do so. His idea was to bowl outside the off stick and dare the batsman to cut him. The inference is, of course, that he was too quick for them to even attempt the stroke. Speed must have been one of the chief weapons in his armoury, and cricket legend has it that he was really fast – some of his contemporaries said the fastest of all. All unwittingly, he had one greater power in his hands. Some people call it conceit; some say that it is a too good opinion of himself; but for my part, I am content to say that it was faith in himself. Kortright had sufficient faith in himself to think that no one could cut him.

Above all else, a quick bowler must have faith in himself: in his ability to bowl faster than anyone else; and in his superiority over the batsman. Those who call it being big-headed know nothing of fast bowling, for this faith in his own ability never allows the real bowler to give up. It drives him on to even greater effort. How many times I have gone back to the end of my run saying (I report in diluted language): 'That was a terrible delivery! Now come on, Frank, you're too quick for this chap. Let's have one a little bit quicker. You can do it.' Perhaps you cannot, but the great fast bowler is the one who never acknowledges defeat. He never knows when he is beaten.

When he bows his head, he is no longer a real quick bowler. Some people call it guts. I prefer to call it the infallibility of the fast bowler.

In cricket I suppose I never really outgrew my childhood values. A fast bowler is like that. Even to the end of my career, everything seemed possible. When Australia wanted almost 200 to win the third Test at Melbourne in 1955, I never dreamt that they would score them. In one's dreams there is always the fairy tale hope of the last minute hat-trick which saves the side. It is a kind of incurable optimism which bears the fast bowler along on a wave of enthusiasm. The match can be won, no matter what the odds. If anyone stands in the way of winning the match, he is the enemy to be hated with an almost childlike intensity. I have often felt that youth captures the spirit of fast bowling, for it is exuberant, self-centred, and full of love-hate complexes. It brooks no half measures; rather it is the world of pure undiluted enthusiasm.

The fast bowler is a dyed-in-the-wool character and to him there can never be a gentle art of quick bowling. It is, rather, a vicious, demanding science. When I bowl fast, I feel that it is something to revel in and to enjoy. Cricket always carries its own rewards and, for me, that reward is the sight of a cartwheeling stump, or the excitement of snick, the half-stifled, half-anticipatory, involuntary appeal, and the sight of the flying wicket-keeper. What a fillip the sight of Godfrey Evans hurling himself at the ghost of a chance gives to a bowler. It has often made me think that Godfrey was a player who put as much into his wicketkeeping as I put into fast bowling. I well remember his catch to dismiss Neil Harvey at Melbourne in 1954. If ever a catch decided the series that was it! Most wicket-keepers find difficulty in seeing the ball all the way when a left-hander is batting to a right-handed bowler. Consequently the keeper has to stand wide on the off-side. Godfrey was a yard outside the off-stick when Harvey, sensing easy runs, flicked a ball off his pads through the gap between wicket-keeper and leg-slip; but suddenly there was no gap – just the flash of a blue cap, a huge glove and the loudest appeal you ever heard! Godfrey came to rest at the feet of Colin Cowdrey, the ball clasped in his midriff. Even the large Colin heaved himself several feet off the ground in elation. After that catch, the capture of the remaining wickets seemed almost easy.

Just as everyone loves to see the fireworks guaranteed by the presence of Godfrey Evans, so everyone seems to like to watch the fast bowler in action. I suppose quick bowling is a side of the game which everyone, no matter how unversed in cricket, can understand. The bouncer always draws the ohs and the ahs from the crowd. I was sitting with Gary Merrill, the American actor, in the course of a charity match, watching a fast bowler perform. Even though he had never seen a game before, Gary was stimulated to say 'Gee, he pitches a mean curve'. You see, there is something basic in the sheer physical quality of fast bowling that appeals to everyone.

I well remember playing in the West Indies with Jim Swanton's team in the winter of 1955-56. The coloured sections of the crowds were remarkably well-informed about their cricket, and offered their advice quite freely. More than any other department they seemed to like fast bowling and were for ever urging me to 'T'ro him down another bouncer'. The team played one match of the tour in Point-à-Pierre, quite close to Sonny Ramadhin's home town of San Fernando. In that game I was lucky enough to hit the stumps four times in quick succession. I have never seen spectators react like it! At one stage the locals on the popular side were literally turning somersaults in the aisles. Here was something they really enjoyed. It was violent, aggressive and easy to watch. No wonder they loved to watch it.

Many people have asked me whether there has ever been a faster bowler than I. It is one of the old favourites, in the same category as 'who is the best batsman you have ever bowled against?' It can also be an embarrassing question. If you have the temerity to say 'No, there has been no faster,' you are immediately branded as a big-head; yet if you say 'Yes' the fault becomes that of excessive modesty. When we were in New Zealand in 1955, Brian Statham and I became the objects of scientific research. By bowling into a radio beam projected the length of a cricket pitch, it was discovered that Brian bowled at 85 m.p.h. and I at 89 m.p.h. I must add, that both Brian and I bowled in two sweaters. Indeed, Brian did not even bother to take off his grey flannels!

So, my stock answer to the question about my pace is: 'Ask the batsman.' He is the one who ought to worry about my pace; for my part, I have never given it much thought. I have spent more time considering the correctness of my action, and trying to right its faults. Harold Larwood gave me a very happy moment in 1954. Even before the first Test, he told me that he thought I should make a fast bowler, because I used my body. After that I felt sure that genuine pace would follow.

I labour under no illusions. I know that there have been better bowlers; greater bowlers, with better actions, more control and greater accuracy. Keats said in one of his letters 'O for a life of sensation rather than thoughts'. That would be a good comment on my bowling; for I have always been a bowler of sensation, who bowled well and fast when he felt right. There were many things in the course of my bowling career that forced me back into mediocrity. The umpire who made me drag from a long way behind the bowling crease often caused me a great deal of embarrassment. Like Alec Bedser, I stretched to reach the wicket, lengthened my stride, and lost rhythm. But if the rhythm was there, the wind behind, and my stride long and flowing, then it was a case of 'watch out, batsmen'.

Oh yes, there have been better fast bowlers. But I doubt whether there has been one who derived more pleasure from bowling fast. One of its greatest attractions for me is its straightforwardness. It is an honest pursuit whose rewards are gained by the sweat of the brow, and not by any underhand or surreptitious methods. The Aussie would say that fast bowling calls a spade a so-and-so shovel. Perhaps it is the directness of quick bowling to the problem of removing the batsman which has caused it to be the centre of so many controversies. In the 1830s there was the argument about roundarm bowlers; the similar problem of throwing still exists today, and we have had the interim disputes about bodyline, bumpers, and drag. Harold Larwood told me that he only had second thoughts about bowling quick on one occasion. It was at Adelaide, during the 'bodyline tour', when the crowd, after several incidents, had just seen Bert Oldfield knocked unconscious, and were just about ready to come over the fence at the 'Poms'. 'If they come after us', said Harold to Les Ames, 'you take the leg stump and I'll take the off, and make for the pavilion.'

For all these minor differences of opinion, fast bowling is essentially an honest enjoyment, and one that brings character into the game. It is said that all wicket-keepers and fast bowlers are mad; and who am I to disagree? I suppose it must seem so when one considers the fast bowlers who have been real characters: the Hopper Reads, George Browns, Nobby Clarkes, and Fred Truemans.

In our own day, an over from Fred Trueman is worth watching, for Fred is not only a great swing bowler, but also a great crowd-pleaser. Even now, weeks after the end of the season, I can still picture Fred on the field; walking back to the end of his run, cowboy-fashion, polishing the ball vigorously on his ample backside: his smooth run and violent action end with him taking up position half-way down the wicket, hands on hips, toes turned inwards and his black forelock hanging over his eyes. Should the batsman play and miss, he is treated to a few minutes of Trueman burlesque; the glare and some pungent remarks. I have seen minutes elapse between the balls of a Trueman over – and how the crowds loved the show! I was told that once when he played for Yorkshire Willie Watson missed a catch off Fred at first slip. There was the usual dramatic pause, which was ended by Willie saying, 'Come on Fred, I've a train to catch.' Fred favoured him with a glance, and said 'Doant worry, lad, tha'll miss it – same as tha' does everything else.' This is the sort of charade spectators love to see on the field, for it gives a flavour to the game.

Too often players allow cricket to sink into the neutral

sepia tint of a nine-to-five job, and as a result become neutral characters themselves. Genuine fast bowlers never sink into this limbo, for real enthusiasm cannot lead to a humdrum existence. No wonder that we find so many characters and personalities among them. They possess a very rare quality; a quality which explains my whole attitude towards fast bowling, my motives and my feelings. They love cricket.

CHAPTER TWO

# Cricket-Crazy Boy

I can hardly say that cricket was in my blood. Neither of my parents showed a great deal of interest in the game. Indeed, in later years, when cricket began to interfere with school work, they did their utmost to persuade me to spend less time with the bat and more with the pen. Happily, I converted them to my way of thinking and eventually they became my greatest fans and, at the same time, my most severe critics.

Though my parents had no cricket ability with which to endow me, they left me one great legacy; my name, Frank Holmes Tyson. I should not have the temerity to claim I was even distantly related to Percy Holmes, but it is a fact that mother was born, and has remained throughout her life, a staunch Yorkshirewoman; while cricket records show that there was a Cecil Tyson who played for Yorkshire and made a hundred on his début. Unfortunately, he hardly ever played first-class cricket again.

My début in the game of cricket came when I was very young. In the words of the old music-hall joke, my fast bowling career was born at a very early age. In his ode on the recollections of early childhood, Wordsworth tells us that we grow away from the truths of youth. Looking back at that time of my life, I find it impossible to remember the continuous thread of events. What I can recollect is a series of highlights; the great events, happy and unhappy, that coloured my early cricket life and seem far removed from the harsh realities of my later life in the game.

I remember that, as children, we used to have crazes. Sometimes it was cigarette cards or conkers, next week it might be marbles; but the main stream of these fashions passed me by. No matter what the time of year, no matter what the current craze, my main occupation – and preoccupation – was cricket. Even at that tender time of my life, I have a hazy recollection of watching league cricket. At the back of my mind is the distant memory of seeing Leary Constantine in action, against a golden background that seemed not only to represent a glorious summer day, but also a cricketer at the height of his powers.

My father was a foreman-bleacher by trade, and he, my mother, my brother David and I lived in a small council house in the town of Middleton, near Manchester. Beyond the concrete fence that marked the limit of our garden there was an open stretch of waste land. Among the kids of the district there was the rumour that the 'back' had been an old coalmine, and there were many gruesome tales of how it came to be derelict. This was my very first cricket pitch. The wicket itself was of grey shale and was amazingly good. Many years later I saw the same material, damped down with diesel oil, being used to surface sports grounds in Aden. Our cricket in those days did not boast two wickets. We batted only at one end, for bats and pads were rare treasures. The stumps were represented by a much-battered, flat-faced oil-drum of the type which gives its name in Australia to 'kerosene-can cricket'. Our ball was a 'corkie' of course. My brother was eight years older than I and played with the older boys; inevitably I tried to gate-crash their circle and, equally inevitably, I was rejected. It is said that W. G. Grace faced a similar problem, and that his companions at net-practice eventually were his sisters. Perhaps this is the only common ground I can claim with the great man, for it was mother who had to compensate for brother David's intractability. On many occasions she had to leave her household chores to bowl at her younger son, who would burst into tears if she left him to his own devices. I think that it came as a great relief to her when I grew to school age and joined cricketing forces with my friend Geoffrey. We would play cricket for hours, just the two of us; each taking turns to bat. Even in those days my first thought was to bowl fast. It was a great sensation to see the tin drum rock back with a hollow boom that could be heard around the whole field. Often Geoffrey protested that I bowled before he was ready and there would be a flaming row. With the naïveté of a child, I thought I was just bowling too fast for him! There was no opposition we would not play, and very few who were too strong for us. Quite often, Geoff and I would shoulder our prize bat, and march off to seek out, play against, and sometimes beat, teams of five or six other boys. We had no cricket season, for it seemed unnecessary. Cricket was, to us, a game to be played at every opportunity and in all kinds of weather.

So I grew up, and the world grew up around me. Touring cricket sides came to, and went from, England without my noticing them. The only name I retained from those days was that of my childhood hero, 'Lol' Larwood. He seemed to personify everything I wanted to be. Then Hitler invited himself on a tour of England. For me it meant the end of cricket for a while. Like many other children all over England I was hustled to the safety of the countryside, away from the bombs which were to fall on our cities. I was in Fleetwood, and the war for me at this early age was represented by the glow of Liverpool burning, far to the south. Even the war could not stop my cricket; indeed it seemed to give me the chance of better cricketing facilities. It was while I was at Fleetwood that I passed my entrance examination for the local grammar school, and for the first time in my life went to a school which had a real cricket pitch. There were nets to practise in, and I remember that one of my favourite ways of keeping my hand in was to bowl at a single stump until I could hit it with at least one in ten balls. Cricket was my ruling passion, and I well remember the domestic upheaval caused by my cousin when in a fit of pique he threatened to chop up my cricket bat!

The war had almost ended when I returned to Middleton, and with it had gone my early childhood. The haze of doubt that surrounded earlier episodes in my life had evaporated, and it is from this time that my cricket development has a definite shape and progression. My former cricket pitch had disappeared beneath a huge Ministry of Fuel coal dump, but I did not worry, for I moved in the realms of real cricket pitches now. I was eleven when I first went to my new school in Middleton. I was eighteen when I left, and in the course of those seven years I had risen to be a minor county cricketer and a university undergraduate. Many years later I returned to the Queen Elizabeth Grammar School and presented a memento of the Australian '54 tour to the headmaster. It was a poor return for what I consider to have been the most formative period of my life, both in cricket and education.

It was a glorious seven years. My summer day was long and full. Each lunch-break was occupied by a two-hour net practice. Even after school we managed an extra hour before going home. How well I remember who 'we' were: Geoff, Tubby, and I: cricket fanatics all, who liked nothing better than to spend the Saturday afternoon at the town cricket ground, perhaps helping to operate the score-board, or keeping tally in our own score-books. For us it was cricket all the way.

At school there were form games, house games, and any other games we could improvise. Out of school I played in games between churches. In those days I used to fancy myself as something of a batsman and I would bat quite high up in the order, on wickets which were slightly tricky, to say the least. Once I made top score for the Providence Sunday School with a magnificent 13 out of a total of 15: but it was not my score that filled me with pride; it was the beautiful black eye I collected in the process of batting!

It is not to be thought that my rise in cricket was meteoric and spectacular throughout my career. In the early days nothing could be further from the truth. I was not chosen to play for the junior school until several weeks after my arrival in Middleton. I was rather piqued by my omission, since all my friends were playing. However the great day arrived when, with a sinking heart, I approached the school notice-board and read: 'Tyson – twelfth man'. I have never indulged in voodoo, or wished evil on any person, but on the Friday before that particular match the whole of the team were in grave danger. If my dearest wish had been granted, at least one of the players would have been struck by bubonic plague, or at the very mildest, a bad cold. I can still recollect carrying the school cricket-bag to the bus-stop, waiting in fear and trepidation in case everyone turned up, and my selfish exultation when the team was one short. This was one of the great first-times in my life: the first time I played in an official cricket match. There was hardly the opportunity to cover myself in glory for we were bowled out for 25, but there was the satisfaction of being top scorer for my side – and taking four wickets, bowling fourth change.

In those distant days I could hardly be classified as a fast bowler. I do not really think I ever thought I should be one of the fastest in the world, though I desperately wanted to be. In my first match, our opponents boasted a really fast young bowler, and it was he who wrought the havoc among our batsmen. I can still see, in my mind's eye, how terrifyingly fast he was, and how slow I was in comparison. In those days my run-up was of the briefest; five jogging paces up to the wicket, and then a quick flurry of arms which hardly seemed to help the ball on the way at all. Of course, I was hardly as heavy or tall as I was at my peak. In many ways I have never regretted my lack of pace as a boy, for it made me concentrate on basic factors; on the importance of keeping my arm high to brush my ear as I bowled, and on the paramount point of correct positioning of the body at the moment of delivery. Too often good potential is wasted in fast bowling by insistence on being second Lindwalls and second Stathams at too callow an age. How often in the parks of England, youngsters tear up to the wicket from a twenty-yard run, with the cry, 'Look, I'm Lindwall'. I think that I put first things first and chose the easier way of becoming a fast bowler. Fast bowling, like Ben Ezra, should bear this advice for the younger generation:

*'Grow old along with me!*
*The best has yet to be.'*

My first school match and our catastrophic defeat had strange results. Being a democratic sort of body, the side had an inquest on the result of the game and, at the end of the wake, there was a bloodless revolution, and I found I had been elected captain for the following game. It had been quite a promotion; from twelfth man to skipper in one game!

We were essentially a cricketing school. At one time there were four representatives in the town side; and one player, a fine left-hander by the name of Jim Hyde, played minor county cricket while still at school. He was a hero of mine when I was in the junior school and I would go out of my way to pass his house on the way to school. There was no lack of keenness in my junior side. Once we went to the extreme of sweeping snow off the wicket to play: only to be disappointed by another snow storm! Each summer we played a full week of cricket after the examinations, and our keenness was such that, if results were anything to judge by, we were second to none.

Summer succeeded summer and, with the passing time, I graduated to the first eleven. In the winters I survived by playing football, and once even represented Lancashire schoolboys. At athletics I was never outstanding, but managed, on the odd occasion, to win a few events. It was my one proud boast that no one ever beat me at throwing the cricket ball. I was already throwing it a hundred yards when I was sixteen.

My passage to first eleven skipper was more of an inheritance than an election. It was well known by this time that I was the school's village idiot about cricket. The season's programme had become very crowded, for now I was a playing member of the Middleton Cricket Club. Each evening of the week, when school had ended, I would tramp home over the cobbled streets, past the house from which one of the ill-fated marches to Peterloo began in 1819. There would be barely time to gulp down some tea, collect my cricket gear and dash off to net practise at the town ground. My preoccupation with the game reached such a pitch that mother was soon worried that it might lead to neglect of my school-work. However, a little hard work at the right time and good school reports soon overcame her objections to cricket.

Saturday at this time of my life was a wonderful day. We played our schoolboy matches in the morning. They were one innings affairs but, even so, it meant a very early start if they were to be finished by midday. At fourteen I was playing regularly for the town second eleven and, since the matches began at 2.30 each Saturday, and quite often the team had to travel away, it meant that lunch was a sketchy and sometimes non-existent meal. Many times I would run over the fields between the school and the town cricket ground with only minutes to spare before the start of my second match of the day.

My first captain in representative cricket was genial

Tom Heywood, town councillor and cricket counsellor. A young cricketer could have had no better sponsor. His build was visual encouragement in itself, for being well into his 'fifties, he was quite rotund; yet he bowled off-spinners with deceptive guile and accuracy. Many of the boys in the team were old-boys of the school. Some played keenly, some turned out for exercise, and some to forget their girl-friends for an afternoon! Together we had some great experiences. In my very first match I was brilliantly stumped by the wicket-keeper, and it was not until the end of the match that I learnt he had a wooden leg! I was very quickly taught that in league circles the cricketer moves in very tough company. Once Middleton second eleven played an away fixture against a village in the foot-hills of the Pennines. It was a pretty little ground, and during the interval there was always the sight of seemingly the whole population of the village in the shafts of the biggest roller I have ever seen, preparing the wicket for the next innings. Of course, if the visitors were batting second, the willing workers all wore the heaviest of boots and clogs! While batting in the game I was called for the quickest of quick singles, to find that half-way down the wicket my path was barred by the bowler, a giant of a man with a frightening black spade beard! By the simple expedient of a slight shoulder movement, I was sent tumbling back down the wicket and run out easily. It was then I realised the truth of the Americanism 'Never give a sucker an even break'.

I wish I could write that I bowled well for my town team, but the truth will out, and I must admit that I was a boy among young men, and my performances reflected my immaturity. I have often wondered if it was my lack of success that made those days so full of enjoyable cricket and happy memories!

I do not suppose that I have received more than a hundred hours' coaching in the whole of my cricket career, and not for a minute do I think that I am the worse for it. The best advice ever given to me was that of the old Middleton professional, Alf Casseley. He took me to one side and asked me how I held the ball. I had not given the matter much thought, but just gripped the ball any old how. 'Son,' said Alf, 'this is how to bowl the outswinger: now go and work it out.' Coaching can be a mixed blessing, for too often the coach tries to create a player either in his own image, or in the uniform image of the M.C.C. manual. The worst possible thing is for a young player to lose the individuality in his play. A good coach accepts the limitations of the individual player and then tries to bend the correct method of play to meet them. I think this is where the M.C.C. coaching manual falls short. Not everyone can play according to figures one, two, and three, and retain his greatness. The spark of genius in Denis Compton was his lack of orthodoxy, and few great players have been completely orthodox. When Peter May was making a coaching film for the M.C.C., he was told by Harry Crabtree, who was directing it, to take up the bat and settle into his stance. When he was standing comfortably at the wicket, Harry turned to him and said, 'What are you doing? You can't possibly stand like that! Put your right hand further behind the bat: now bring the left elbow further round . . . ' and he proceeded to rearrange Peter May's natural stance, which had already brought him almost 3,000 runs that year! It was not correct according to the book.

If I were to give any advice to young players it would be – 'Listen to me. Listen to anyone who will give you advice. When you stop learning, you have finished playing. When you have listened, go away and, as Alf Casseley said to me, "Work it out." Find out the best way to apply the advice to your own game.'

I suppose if anyone had offered me advice when I was fourteen years old, I should not have listened very attentively. I was far too engrossed in the glamour of cricket to realise it requires any hard work or concentration. I was never a great watcher of first-class cricket – even in later years, I could not watch the whole of the game from the dressing-room windows – but two games at Old Trafford are clear in my mind.

The first time I visited Old Trafford was on the occasion of a Roses match shortly after the war. As a Lancastrian, I find it difficult to express how much I had looked forward to seeing the encounter with the hated rival, Yorkshire. The ground was almost full on this, the day of my first – and last – Roses match. What a dismal day's cricket it was! I had been reading Cardus, and my sentiments were entirely on the side of the gentleman in the bowler hat, who is described in my fellow-Lancastrian's writings as upbraiding Mitchell, the Yorkshire batsman, with – 'What, art still theer! Well, I'll tell thee somaat, Mitchell, it's nineteen-thirty-nine and theer's a war comin', so tha' won't be theer next year!' I have never had the slightest wish to see another Roses match.

My second visit to Old Trafford was in 1945 to see the Victory Test. The ground was crowded and, as a youngster, I naturally found my way on to the grass verge. For days I watched the cricket, and gazed at the immaculate flannels of the passing parade of players at fine leg. There I was, squatting on the grass, beneath the city-end scoreboard, literally and metaphorically at the feet of my heroes. The facts and figures of the match escape me, but I shall always remember the long loping run of George Pope bowling from the city end, and the towering hook for six which the Aussie Bob Cristofani put through the members' window in the pavilion. Many years later I met Bob when he was Australian Trade Commissioner in South Africa, and reminded him of this mighty blow. Keith Miller played in the Victory Tests and I remember being amazed by the shortness of his run when I saw him on the next Australian tour of England. In 1945 Nugget bowled from a tremendous run and his pace and inaccuracy were in proportion. He was really fast and all over the place.

The highlight of the match was the dismissal of Pepper. Len Hutton was at deep third man when the Australian batsman played the ball in his direction and called for two. The Yorkshireman picked up with one hand and flung down the one visible stump from a full seventy yards! I knew Cec Pepper in later years, and often wondered what his comment was when he reached the dressing-room again.

I little realised, as I watched these giants of the cricket field, that within ten years I should be one of their number, and little boys would be eyeing me with the same awe, and asking for my autograph. Not for a moment did I think I was destined to play cricket before a crowd of 60,000. The years of apprenticeship had not even begun, but they were just around the corner.

CHAPTER THREE

# League Cricket and Personalities

As a boy it was never very difficult to find me on most evenings. Four out of every seven nights I was bowling at the nets. On the fifth I was bowling in a match.

I never even saw the club committee gather at the back of the net as I bowled at one of the Middleton first team batsman, and not for a moment did I realise I was being considered for the town eleven. They told me of my promotion as I was complacently watching the second team play Castleton Moor. My large cricket boots were perched on the seat in front, my eyes almost closed. 'Frank', said the skipper 'you're playing for the first against Royton on Monday.' There was a thud as my size eights hit the ground. I had not turned in any performances to warrant my selection. It could not have come as a greater surprise. Nevertheless it was my opportunity and I was determined to grasp it with both hands.

I was fifteen when I first took part in top-class league cricket, and from the very first I seemed destined for a spectacular rise. Yet although my début was a thrilling affair for me, it was at the same time a chastening experience. It made me realise that in the cricket world success is not handed out on a platter.

Middleton batted first and unfortunately we received rough treatment at the hands of the Royton bowlers. The total had only just topped seventy when I, the last hope of the side, went to the wicket, and left it not having troubled the scorers. In 'bagging' my duck I had learnt my first cricket lesson. The very first ball I received reared nastily from a full length, and seemed to be about to hit me in the mouth. I just managed to protect myself with a flurry of gloves and bat, inches in front of my face, and sighed with relief as the ball was deflected, and disappeared into the unknown. The fieldsmen began to gather round and ask solicitously if I was all right. Apparently they were under the impression that the ball had hit me in the throat or chest. I assured them all was well and I had not been hit. The bowler would have gone back to his mark to bowl the next ball, had I not chosen that precise moment to begin wringing the hand that had been struck. Of course, there was a quiet appeal, and the umpire gave me out.

There are pavilion critics on every field. In the Central Lancashire League it seemed they used to sit in the front row of the enclosure. As I was leaving the field with the inevitable nought appearing on the score-board, a cloth-capped head wagged at me from the usual place and an old gaffer sucked his clay pipe as he spoke. 'Nay, lad,' he said, 'that'll larn thee: next time, rub thi' chest.' The lesson was well taken.

Throughout the tea-interval I was terrified with the thought: 'What if my bowling is as unsuccessful as my batting?' All my friends were watching, and it seemed I should never be able to face them again. The idea continued to torment me as the regular opening bowler sent down the first over. When he had finished, I almost wished that the captain would not throw the ball to me; but he did. It was hard and slippery and almost fell from my hands. It came home to me suddenly that I had never bowled before with a new ball. Carefully I measured out my run: one, two, three, four, five paces. Inwardly I was telling myself: 'Don't try to bowl too fast in the first over.' Off came my sweater. I went back to the end of my short run, took a deep breath and I was off. In those days my pace was medium, and gave no indication that it would develop to be fast. My approach to the wicket was slow. I picked my way gently to the stumps with five short finicky steps before my body braced itself violently, rocked back as if trying to touch the ground behind, and my arm flailed over.

The first ball seemed to wobble just as it reached the bat, which had been extended in a forward defensive prod. It eluded the outside edge, tickled the off-stump without disturbing it, and the off-bail fell gently to the ground. I had taken a wicket with my very first ball. What a wonderful beginning! It seemed miraculous to me that a ball could swing so late in its flight. I had always been used to the even movement of the old ball that we used in lesser matches. The first three deliveries were outswingers. It was then that I decided to try the inswinger, a ball which I had only recently added to my armoury. I approached the wicket almost warily, and without guile I stepped wide on the bowling crease and pushed the ball in at the batsman. Reg Parkin, the Royton professional, played inside it, and as the ball rapped him on the pads, I leapt high in the air with a rapturous appeal. The umpire's finger stabbed upwards and I realised, as if waking from an anaesthetic, that I had taken another wicket.

The match was an evening fixture played on two consecutive nights, and at close of play on the first day I had the remarkable analysis of 4 for 12. Next day I had no further success, but I found consolation in the fact that Middleton won by 20 runs.

The Central Lancashire League was my cricket school for the next six years. It was a comprehensive education, and one that fitted me for the task to come. I have taken part in many arguments about which school provides the better young cricketers: the leagues or the county staffs. Give me the leagues every time. They turn out a player not only technically equipped, but also seasoned in the rough-and-tumble of hard competitive cricket. No wonder Yorkshire and Lancashire have the edge on many counties in young players. Their colts have been playing in league cricket against top professionals for years before they come into first-class cricket. Many of the tailor-made players who came to my adopted county of Northamptonshire hailed from the League, and they were admirable material for a team which did not want to spend too long in grooming them for professional cricket.

In the northern leagues one plays against the cream of the world's cricketers. One week George Tribe bowled me out with his googly; next week Hazare thrashed my bowling all over the field. I remember playing against Charlie Barnett in his very first match for Rochdale and being amazed at the way he hit the ball with a flat bat over the top of cover's head off the opening bowlers. To be precise, I ought to say that I was the bowler!

However there are moments of satisfaction for the youngster who plays against these gods, and more than once I succeeded in giving the opposing professional a severe shock. Cecil Pepper has long been one of the most serviceable of league professionals, as well as one of the leading wags, and on one occasion Middleton played against his team of Rochdale, when Cec was in one of his purple patches with the bat. As is the case on such occasions the whole of the town of Rochdale was hanging on Pepper's next innings. He strode to the wicket after the first man had been dismissed in the first over, his burly figure almost the shape of the nought which stood against his team's total on the score-board. Taking guard he looked purposefully around the field, and then settled down into his stance as I cantered up to bowl. There was a large crowd watching, as it was a round of the local knock-out Wood Cup. I wonder if Cec realised that a slip of a boy could bowl fast. He was only just picking up his bat as a really fast one sent his middle stick cartwheeling spikily into the wicket-keeper's gloves. As Pepper walked back to the pavilion the silence was deafening: the stunned quietness of disappointment.

Not all the stories of Cecil Pepper are of disappointment. I remember the time when a batsman was having a lean time playing against the Australian's leg-spinners and googlies. On six separate occasions in one over he played at the ball and missed. The call of 'Over' must have come as a relief to him. Looking up, he saw that Pepper was coming down the wicket to him. When he drew level with the batsman, he tapped him on the shoulder. 'All right,' he said, 'you can open your eyes now, I've finished.'

I was by far the youngest player in the Middleton side, six years junior to the next youngest man. Indeed, I was a boy amongst men. My team-mates were continually telling me that if I ever wanted to grow-up into a real fast bowler, I should drink the odd glass of beer; but it was too adult a taste for me and remained so until I was over twenty. Quite often the men of the team would tease me about my youth. 'You're too young to play cricket,' they would say.

'You were playing for Middleton when you were my age,' was my answer.

'But things were different in those days. They let me play because they could send someone for a sixpenny jug of beer. Here's sixpence, go and buy a jug.'

So the exchanges would go on.

The spectators, too, were quick to notice the young lad on the field. Although I was big, I was not heavy, and so I had a gawky appearance that made me look exceptionally tall. One Saturday I was batting with my fellow fast bowler, Cliff Evans. Cliff was an ex-Guardsman and over 6 feet 4 in his stockings. In the course of our characteristically short partnership I failed to ground my bat at one end. The umpire immediately called 'One short'. A spectator on the popular side shouted: 'Where? They both look over six foot to me.'

Since my early days I have been to many places throughout the world: I have played before crowds of many nations and colours. But nowhere in the world have I ever come across such discerning and humorous people as those who watch Lancashire League cricket. The Australian is a consistently noisy barracker, always ready to come out with the well-worn shout, 'You'll never get 'im out: send for the fire brigade, they'll put 'im out.' But occasionally the Australian crowd will produce a brilliant quip, as they did once when I was bowling at Sydney. In my early days, my run was over twenty yards, and it took quite a while to bowl an over; a situation that pleased the bowler at the other end, but quickly irritated the spectators. One day, after about twenty interminable overs, a watcher on the Sydney Hill could bear it no longer and, just as I was returning to the end of my run somewhere near the pickets he leapt to his feet, and shouted at the top of his voice:

'I don't know where you're going, Tyson, but the Gents are over 'ere!'

The West Indian is, on the other hand, an ebullient bubbling spectator who almost reveres his cricketing heroes. When one Indian member of our team walked into a café or restaurant in Trinidad, where there is a large Indian population, the music would stop and he would be presented to the clientèle:

'Ladies and gentlemen, the management have great pleasure in introducing Mr Swaranjhit Singh of the Swanton cricket team.'

The Lancashire League spectator is amusing without being noisy and enthusiastic without being carried away. When I was watching a league match, one of my friends was batting and not having a very happy time. Off the first ball he received he was dropped in the slips; the second almost had him leg before; and the third sent his middle-stump rocketing out of the ground. I suppose he was feeling pretty sorry for himself, and his mood was not improved by the comment of one of his friends who tapped him on the shoulder and said: 'Eh, Edwin, tha' were lucky to make nowt!'

This sort of leg-pulling was an everyday occurrence for me, but in spite of all the teasing I endured about my youth, Middleton did manage to win the Wood Cup in 1948 with my assistance. At the time I was almost a grown man of seventeen!

Already, in my late 'teens, I was considerably faster than when I first began league cricket. My run-up had been lengthened to nine paces and my speed had increased so much that I began to wonder whether I was trying to bowl too fast. I was still growing and I began to suffer the usual fast bowler's crop of pulled muscles.

However, I carried on undeterred, and once more helped Middleton to reach the final of the Wood Cup. It was against Ashton, as I remember, and at one stage it seemed we were going to win easily. Very quickly, I had two of their batsmen back in the pavilion, only to see countless chances to the slips missed and the match elude our grasp. Nothing is more exasperating to a fast bowler than missed catches in the slips: nothing, that is, except a could-not-care-less expression on the face of the culprit. For me, even the sheepish or contrite transgressor is not enough. I would far sooner see a player genuinely angry with himself, and determined that it will not happen again.

With advancing experience in the league came an increasing number of acquaintances. When I look back on those years, I am amazed by the host of players I bowled and batted against, who since then have played either county or test cricket. Jack Dyson and Peter Marner played for Lancashire – Geoff Pullar and Malcolm Hilton for England, too. Brian Statham turned out for Stockport, and when he and I were in Australia, we compared notes on the subject. Apparently we missed playing against one another as long ago as 1949 because of injury and national service. From what I know of Brian's bowling and my batting, I am rather relieved.

Of all the players produced by the league: of all the

Ken Grieves and Alan Whartons, Keith Andrew remains highest in my regard. This is entirely natural; I have played all my county professional career in his company, and he has remained one of my best friends. Yet in many ways he has always been an enigma, and I could never quite fathom him. I know, and many other capable judges know, that for the past three years Keith has been the best equipped 'keeper, technically, in the country; yet he has just fallen short of public recognition as a great 'keeper. He seems to have lacked the spark of obvious genius which stamped such men as Godfrey Evans. This first match in which both Keith and I took part will remain stamped on my memory. The scene was the Didsbury cricket ground just outside Manchester, and the Central Lancashire League was playing the Manchester Association. The first catch Keith took off my bowling soon convinced me of his ability behind the stumps, but it was his attitude to batting which really amazed me. In those days he was a batsman of no mean repute, as his friends in the North will bear out, and he used to open the innings for his club. On this day he went in first, and after making a very attractive 20 runs, danced down the wicket and was quite unnecessarily stumped. The skipper, a fellow-clubmate of Keith's, was furious.

'Why did you get out in that stupid way?' he demanded.

'Ah,' said Keith, 'I wanted to see whether I could play the bowling, and when I found I could, I thought there was no point staying there!'

I am glad to say that, since he began playing first-class cricket, Keith's attitude to batting has undergone a radical change, but at heart he remains what he has always been; a self-perfectionist. It does not matter who is watching the game, or who is sitting in judgment on his wicket-keeping, Keith continues to play to the high standards of his own code. More than anyone else I have met in contemporary cricket, he has evolved his department of the game into a fine science, and plays it for his own enjoyment and to his own perfectionist satisfaction. He is so involved in his private thoughts and judgment that it is difficult to carry on conversation with him. An inquiry does not guarantee a reply for perhaps a full five minutes, and often he will begin a statement, only to forget what he is talking about before the end of the sentence. Sitting by his side on a coach trip once, I noticed that he was unusually silent. Later it transpired that he was counting the telegraph poles as they flew past, timing the intervals, and working out the speed of the bus!

Many people criticise him for his lack of show, the quality of liveliness behind the wickets that can infuse new life into a team. Unobtrusiveness is his nature, but he is not a worse wicket-keeper for it. In my career he has backed me up to the hilt, and I say hail to him, the absent-minded professor of wicket-keepers.

CHAPTER FOUR

# The Steps to County Cricket

I doubt if the army personnel selection officer was very surprised by my answer. He must have interviewed hundreds that day who, when they were asked what they most wanted to do in the army, replied that they just wanted to get out. To tell the truth, I was a little annoyed because National Service came at a very awkward time for me. My main ambition when I was eighteen was to go to university, but colleges were giving preference to students who had already served in the forces. So I found myself whirled into the khaki vortex of the Royal Signals and Catterick Camp. A few months later I was not so sure about my earlier answer to the personnel selector, for I found a sportsman's life in the army was not so bad after all. Indeed, I began to regret that I had only one summer to spend in the Services. Strangely enough the army cricket system proved to be one of the most democratic organisations in which it has ever been my pleasure to play. The simple rule was that if you were good enough, you played for the regiment; if your performances warranted it, promotion to the garrison side followed. So the sequence continued; from garrison to corps; from corps to command; and finally from command to the army side. In the days of 1948 there were very few young first-class professional cricketers in the forces; when elevation to the representative side came for me, most of my team-mates were regular commissioned officers. I often have a chuckle when I look back over those score-sheets, to see the side captained by a Major-General and the next highest rank to my own humble signalman, a captain! Since those days I have met many of my army cricketing friends in the most unexpected places all over the world; from Alan McFadyan running a haulage firm in the remote south of New Zealand, to Brian Gomm, now an industrial manager in Melbourne. It proves what wonderful links of companionship the game of cricket welds.

When I finally settled on a trade to occupy my time in the army, I was told that I had volunteered to be an O.K.C. To the uninitiated, I must explain that this is an abbreviation for Operator Keyboard and Cipher. If you are still in the dark, an Operator Keyboard and Cipher is a teleprinter operator who also codes messages. To most of my cynical army friends, Operator Keyboard and Cipher quickly became Operator Keyboard and Cricketer. It was fair comment, for I was playing cricket during the summer of 1949 for the full seven days a week. It was nothing for me to turn out for five different army sides on five consecutive days.

On one of the rare occasions when I was in barracks, I was bound for the cricket ground when I was halted in my tracks by a tremendous roar behind me.

'That man,' said the voice, 'come here!'

I turned to see a gentleman who looked rather like a sergeant-major.

'Who are you, Corporal?' he said, 'and what are you doing in my squadron's barracks?'

'I'm Corporal Tyson,' I managed to answer, and then added, 'Sir.'

'Oh, you're him, are you,' roared the Bomber, as we called him. 'Well, I'm your new sergeant-major, and though you're one of my instructors, and there are only fifteen of you, I haven't seen *you* since I came here seven weeks ago!'

The simple truth was that I had been playing cricket continuously for seven weeks or more.

While I was in the army I played for the first time against a first-class county. Every Lancastrian cherishes a hope that one day he will play against the traditional rival Yorkshire. Strangely my chance came, not for Lancashire, but for the army side.

It was a damp gloomy week-end; our small hotel was dismal; and the very first person I met on the threshold was a tall lugubrious Guardsman. Many years later I was to know him much better, for this was Alan Oakman, the Sussex opening batsman who shared a room with me on the M.C.C. tour of South Africa in 1956. He had every reason to be unhappy, because the Guards at that time were busy transporting meat during one of the periodic strikes at Smithfield. Normally Alan is a happy soul, and gave me many amusing moments. During the South African tour he was thought to be suffering from a slipped disc, and was laid on an infernal traction machine to stretch him. The trouble was that he was already 6 feet 4 inches tall – and it was horrible to think how big he would be when he rose from his rack! The players said that if he became any taller he would be able to play forward to bouncers! Unknown to anyone, Alan periodically became tired of lying on his back, slipped out of his harness and said to me, 'Come on, let's go down town for the afternoon.' Later it was discovered that his injury was not a slipped disc at all but a foreign body in his back!

The army side played Yorkshire at Hull in 1948. The match was ruined by rain, but it was nonetheless interesting for me, since it gave me a preview of two players of whom I have since seen a great deal. The Tykes had a young fast bowler playing for them: a boy of sixteen or seventeen, stockily built and with a shock of black hair which continually fell over his eyes as he bowled. His run was a smooth acceleration to the wicket and his action was wonderful. This was Fred Trueman in one of his first matches. In those days Fred had developed the habit of flinging back his head just as he bowled and, since he was gazing directly up into the air as he delivered, his direction was erratic. In spite of his lack of accuracy, it was obvious that even at such an early age, he was a great fast bowler in the making. Already he was, by repute, something of a character. When he played in a pre-season Yorkshire match near the city of York, he generated an amount of pace never before experienced by his amateur opponents. After he had disposed of a couple of batsmen pretty quickly, his captain signalled to Fred that he ought to take it easy and give each of the batsmen a run off the mark. The next sacrifice was an elderly ex-colonel complete in I Zingari cap. Fred eyed him down the wicket.

'Tha' all reet,' he said. 'T'skipper says I've to give you one off the mark.' The colonel breathed a visible sigh of relief; but Fred's black brow beetled as he added: 'Then next ball, I'm going to pin you against the so-and-so sight screen.'

The other young player on view in that army game of

1948 was Brian Close. He was still wearing his school uniform, but already an accepted and tried Yorkshire player; indeed, within a season he was selected for England and for a tour of Australia. Had he bothered to work out his game, I am convinced that Brian Close could have been one of the best players of our time. I have never seen a player time the ball better than Close in full flight. Once, in a magnificent histrionic performance, he took 160 off the touring West Indian side whilst batting for the M.C.C. with a pulled leg-muscle. He hit several sixes, without apparent effort, off his one good leg. If only he had *learnt* – and had cut out his sweep shot in Australia in 1950.

Of all the thrills army cricket gave me, the greatest was playing at headquarters, on the sacred turf of Lord's. There are many grounds the world over which send the wonderful tremor of excitement up a player's spine. For me there is none in the world to touch the human quality of the Melbourne Cricket Ground. To sit in the dressing-room there, knowing that outside in the arena over 60,000 people are waiting to watch you play cricket, is a terrifying sensation. If you are a cricketer who loves to play in beautiful surroundings, then the Adelaide Oval or Newlands at Cape Town are your grounds. Adelaide has the ecclesiastical benediction of St Peter's cathedral, and the pervading proximity of the Lofty ranges, while at Newlands evening shadows creep slowly over the ground from the beautiful blue bulk of the dominating Table Mountain. But at Lord's there is a cricket atmosphere; a knowledge that when you play there, you are playing on a ground which is more than a stretch of turf on which cricket is played. It is almost possible to *feel* cricket history rising from the centuries-old turf. I have been to many countries and played on many grounds, but whenever I returned to Lord's, I always felt the same mixed thrill of dread, reverence, and excitement.

Yet funnily enough Lord's holds very few outstanding memories for me. At first I was most unpleasantly influenced by the atmosphere of the Long Room and the attitude of its denizens. Keith Andrew and I laugh when we recollect our first brush with an aristocratic old gentleman on the steps of the Long Room. We were new players to the first-class game and as we made our way off the field for lunch, our path was barred by a venerable member who presented an eyeglass to his face, peered at us, and remarked:

'Ah, and which ones are these?'

I can assure you that, to our equalitarian northern minds, this reference to us as though we were so many prize cattle did not go down too well!

It is a strange fact that I have never played in a Test Match at Lord's. It always seemed that I was injured or not selected, but I can recall several pleasing moments there. Perhaps the most significant occurred in my very first match at headquarters, playing for the army. I had captured a quick wicket in my early overs, and the first-wicket batsman was on his way out of the pavilion. He was a slim young man, immaculately turned out and with his hair brushed well back. As a youth he had batted brilliantly for his public school, Charterhouse, and the school coach, George Geary, said that he was destined to play for England. I shall never forget to my dying day that he wore a pair of pale green spiked batting gloves, a colour which I particularly disliked. My first few balls to the new batsman were delivered from close to the stumps.

The fourth was bowled from the edge of the crease and imagine my delight when the batsman padded up and his off-stick slumped sickeningly back. Such was my meeting with Peter May; the score-sheet read: 'Writer P.B.H. May, bowled Tyson . . . o'.

My bowling seemed to have matured by 1948, and I was striking a genuine fast-medium pace. My run-up, like Topsy, just growed and growed, but even now it was no longer than thirteen steps. The run-up is the peculiar characteristic of each individual fast bowler; they have differing lengths, different rhythms, and quite distinctive appearances. My approach to the wicket has changed a number of times in my career, but never in style or basic rhythm. The main variation has been in length and for many different reasons I have often lengthened or shortened it at different times. After the first Test at Brisbane in 1954 I cut down my 25 yards to a mere 15 with disastrous results – for Australia. On that occasion the heat caused me to reduce it. There have been other reasons which made me add several yards to my approach. The chief of these were, firstly a desire for greater speed and, at other times, that bugbear of fast bowlers – injury. Even off a short run, I have always been able to bowl very fast; but a short run necessarily entails a slow approach to the sticks, and even though the body action may be violent and fast, there is almost no follow-through. If the fast bowler does not run down the wicket, it means that his front leg and his body are taking the full shock of the delivery. It is like firing an artillery gun from a fixed mounting, without any recoil devices; sooner or later something in the gun will snap. So with the fast bowler, if there is no recoil device, his muscles will snap.

When pulled muscles began to trouble me, I simply invented a mechanism to take the shock of my violent body action. Lengthening my run-up meant that I moved faster at the moment of delivery, and quickening my approach automatically lengthened my follow-through. In later years, I have now no doubt that I overdid the extension process and my run ceased to be efficient. Particularly in hot climates, it used up too much energy. When that stage was reached, it was time for cutting-back the excessive growth which threatened to kill the plant.

Many people find it strange that I, a Lancastrian, should play for the midland county of Northamptonshire. To the many inquirers I reply that the fault is not mine. If, in my youth, there was a desire I cherished as much as the wish to play for England, it was an ambition to play for Lancashire. If the Lancashire committee cursed the fact that I left my native county, they had only themselves to blame, for it was they who allowed me to go.

By the time I was seventeen, Old Trafford was taking notice of my league performances. Already I had played for Manchester Schoolboys and acquitted myself so well that it was decided to invite me to the Lancashire nets.

It was an awe-inspiring occasion for a boy of seventeen. When I entered the pavilion at Old Trafford, it was like entering some holy shrine. I felt lonely. Yet outside at the nets everything was different. Here I was in my element and here I had friends. I remember that there was Eric Price to give me encouragement and advice. As a young player he hailed from Middleton and he was now second string to Bill Roberts on the Lancashire ground staff.

While I was changing I was told that there were two

other young hopefuls on trial that day. When I had carefully measured out my nine-pace run, I cast around, looking for my fellow-trialists. They were nowhere to be seen. True, there were two individuals behind me in the near distance, but surely they did not bowl off such long runs. Even as I watched they thundered some twenty yards to the wicket and hurled the ball down at the batsman. They seemed uncomfortably fast.

The batsman, for his part, was making heavy weather of them. His face seemed familiar and when I looked a second time I discovered that it was Phil King. Only the week before I had watched as he cut and carved his way to a valuable century against the most hated of rivals, Yorkshire. The net wicket was fast and very rough. At the end of five minutes, my companions and I had hit the batsman several times on the hands, and he was far from being in a good temper. He flung down the bat, stormed from the net, and John Kelly – the young groundstaff boy and later a Derbyshire player – was compelled to take his place. We were fast enough to give John several anxious moments on this unpleasant wicket. As I walked back to the pavilion, someone tapped me on the shoulder. Looking round, I found it was a small, elderly man dressed in white flannels, a Lancashire blazer and a Lancashire first eleven cap. I was not to know it until later, but this was Harry Makepeace, the chief coach.

'Could I have a few words with you, son?' he said.

He led me to the head of the entrance stairs to the ladies' stand. On the field below, the tourist match was being played and since it was 1947, the visitors were South Africa. Even as we looked on, Alan Melville scored the runs which brought him his century.

'You know,' said Harry Makepeace to me, 'if you come to Old Trafford, I think that I can make you an England bowler.' I thought he must be mad, and when I found out who he was, I thought that I must have been hearing things. It was hard to believe that the coach thought that I was by far the fastest of the three trialists and that Lancashire had room for me on the ground staff.

As I boarded the bus which took me home, my head was in the clouds. Lancashire wanted me! It was too good to be true! It only took five minutes' conversation with my father to bring me down to earth again. He soon made it abundantly clear that under no circumstances would he allow me to go into professional cricket when it was possible for me to go to university. The whole edifice of my cricket ambitions seemed to tumble about my ears.

Yet, as I look back, I thank my father wholeheartedly for that decision. I should never allow a son of mine to enter a sporting profession without first ensuring that he had some other qualification. In the first instance, the sportman's career is a short one, and I personally would want a job that would guarantee security beyond my thirty-fifth or fortieth year. Secondly, it is far from certain that the player who turns to professional cricket will be good enough to command a regular place in a county side. Even if he does, the first-class cricketer can hardly be said to command a princely salary. In this age of falling gates, most clubs shrink from paying salaries in proportion to the rising wages of other jobs. Only when a cricketer is at the top of the tree is the game financially rewarding; it is then that he begins to rake in the advertising fees and bat-royalties. But cricket's rewards do not lie in the pocket-book or wallet; they lie in the comradeship and enjoyment of the game. I have enjoyed every minute I have played, but I have never been totally dependent on the game for a livelihood. Nothing can be worse than to reach the age of forty and to be aware that one's cricket career is ending, and there is nothing to take its place. How can it be a pleasure to play cricket knowing that such a reckoning lies at the end of the road?

To those who contemplate playing professional first-class cricket, I say this. Make sure that you are not totally dependent on cricket for a living; but if you want to play, let nothing stop you. Simply do not gamble with your livelihood.

Though I was not permitted to stake my future on county cricket, I was not cast aside immediately by Lancashire. At the beginning of each season there is a trial match at Old Trafford, a game in which the whole of the professional staff take part. An invitation to play in the pre-season game was extended to me and, though I did not set the town alight with my performances, I was more than satisfied with the scalps of three first-team players. The wickets of Jack Ikin, Winston Place, and John Kelly only cost me 28 runs. In the light of the trial match and the fact that already the name Tyson was beginning to appear on the army team sheet, I was offered a game for Lancashire 2nd XI against Northumberland.

I remember the game well, for it was destined to be the only one I ever played for a Lancashire side. In the summer of 1949 the whole country was disrupted by a series of rail strikes; imagine my horror when I learnt that a stoppage was due to start on the evening before my eagerly anticipated appearance for the county second eleven. On the day before the great game I was playing for an army side in York, and my problem was how to make my way from York to Manchester overnight. The strike began on time and at eight o'clock on the eve of the match I was sitting on my cricket bag on York station, hoping wistfully that there would be a train going my way. After various journeyings to-and-fro over the breadth of Yorkshire and Lancashire, I accomplished the 80-mile journey in 8 hours. Shortly after three in the morning, I tumbled out of the train and began the walk of five miles to my home, still carrying my cricket bag. It never crossed my mind to take a taxi; cabs were out of reach of my army pay. I was in bed by five and the start of the match was only six hours away. I hardly need add that I was late. The bus seemed interminably slow, and though I ran all the way from the bus-stop, still clutching my heavy cricket bag, Lancashire were just taking the field as I dashed into the dressing-room. Seated in a corner was a rotund, ruddy-faced man with grey hair combed smoothly back. For fully ten minutes he treated me to a lecture telling me why I should not be late for such an important match. I agreed, but much to the detriment of my frame of mind, I was not allowed to give my reasons. Later I discovered that I had been talking to the old England wicket-keeper, George Duckworth. If I was annoyed when I ran on to the field ten minutes late, imagine how I felt when, after bowling five overs, I pulled a muscle in the back and left the game for good! That is the brief history of my one and only game for Lancashire, for I never trod the turf of Old Trafford again as a Lancashire player. The secretary was sympathetic, and asked me to write to him when I was fit once more. That was destined to be a long time, for ill-luck seemed to dog me. I sprained my ankle, and then broke my leg playing soccer. I am of the opinion that by the time I was fit once again, the county club had the firm idea that I was injury-prone, even though my aches and pains had not been connected in any way with cricket.

When I had regained full health once more, another cricket season was already under way. In June 1951 I wrote to ask for a game with Lancashire 2nd XI. I received the reply in July. It said briefly:

Dear Tyson,

Thank you for your letter. I am sorry to say that I am afraid I cannot be of any help to you this year. We have extended invitations for the remaining second eleven matches this season, and this, with our existing professional staff, means that there will be no opportunity for you this season.

Yours sincerely,

G. Howard.

I have kept the letter, for I am a sentimentalist. You see, I never heard again from the county cricket club.

For months after my rebuff, I mused bitterly that cricket in England is a closed shop, and that the door of opportunity had been shut politely but firmly in my face. Ever since that time I have never ceased to wonder about the number of top-class cricketers we never see on our cricket fields purely because of our cricket system. Our county selectors must miss thousands, and there must be just as many players who cannot afford to give six days each week to playing cricket. The simple truth is that, in England, there is not a gradual progression and promotion from club to county and England status. There is a sharp and terrible gap between our club players and the full-time county cricketers. At some time in his cricket career the player who is good enough decides whether he is going to devote the whole of his summers to cricket. Once the decision is taken, the ordinary club cricketer is not considered to be eligible for county selection. He simply passes from the ken of first-class cricket. To my mind this means that, for various reasons, personal and professional, England only realises fifty per cent of her full cricket potential.

Though I seemed to be a reject as far as county cricket was concerned, I was soon to learn that I could earn money out of the game. Many league clubs are allowed the stiffening backbone of one professional player, and in the summer of 1951, I was such a player to Knypersley in the North Staffordshire League. The job was a godsend. Father had died while I was in the army, and playing professional cricket seemed a very agreeable way of working my way through college; but right from the first fate seemed determined to place obstacles in the way. I had left the army and had been at Hatfield College, Durham, for exactly one month when I broke my left leg playing soccer. In a way it was rather ironical. I was playing right back at the time and our opponents were Catterick Garrison. I had formerly played cricket for them and, indeed, the officer-in-charge of the football team was my former commanding officer! The blow was all the harder because the left leg is the one that receives all the hard jarring work of a fast bowler's action. By dint of some hard training, I honoured my first professional engagement, but the mended bone was so soft that, ever since that time it has been curved like a long-bow, as a result of the constant pounding.

Many pro players have tried to mix football and cricket. It was not until I broke my leg that I realised how silly this is. Denis Compton tried to play both games, and a football injury made him retire from cricket when he was good for at least another five years of Test Matches. Willie Watson and Arthur Milton also tried to play the two games concurrently but, fortunately, they both saw the danger signal while there was still time and got out of football. The facts are that a batsman can earn a living from cricket until he is forty. The footballer normally finishes in his thirties. The important question is: why sacrifice cricket on the altar of football? Like oil and water, cricket and soccer do not mix, and if the blend is tried, the result is often explosive, as I found out to my cost.

Every Friday evening of my next summer was taken up in travelling from Durham to Stoke. The Saturdays were occupied in playing cricket and the Sunday mornings in journeying back to college. It was a strenuous time and also an important one in my cricket development. For the first time I was playing as a professional, and it really mattered to me *materially* that I should do well. True, money was not my motive for playing cricket; I still played because I enjoyed it – but the fact that I should probably be better rewarded for a better performance drew out the little extra effort. For the first time it was essential that I should do well.

I did do well. In my very first match, while not fully fit, I took five wickets for eight runs. It was an exciting start to what proved to be a glorious season for me.

When September came around, Knypersley were top of their league and, with the very last match of the year, I had the chance of taking a hundred wickets in my first season. Crewe were the visitors, and needing all ten wickets to reach my goal, I failed by two. If anything is to be judged from mere figures, I had a wonderful year. Even with the bat I averaged thirty per innings.

My first season as a professional was a considerable experience. It not only introduced me to a new attitude towards cricket, but brought me into contact with another race of cricketers. I do not think it would be an exaggeration to say that when I first played in Staffordshire I could not understand a word the natives were saying! It was strange how little resemblance playing in the Staffordshire League bore to cricketing in Lancashire. The organisation and arrangement of the two leagues were similar, but the variable factor was the players themselves. It is hard to generalise about people, but I think the Boons and Butlers of the Midland county had a fire that contrasted violently with the phlegmatic quiet humour of the Lancashire people I was used to. I remember how amazed I was by the number of Pottery players who, after trifling differences of opinion with their club, would shift their allegiance to the neighbouring team. And then – within a month of my début in the Staffordshire League, I had been run out – backing up!

'Don't worry lad,' said one of my team-mates, 'we'll fix him.'

The offender was promptly run out in the same way, and honour was satisfied!

I suppose it was inevitable that my university studies suffered because of my weekly jaunts to Stoke, and it was no surprise to me when my tutor decided to put an end to them. Ironically enough, his veto gave me a chance to play more cricket, since I was free to take part in the various college matches. Nearly every summer afternoon found me on the college cricket ground, a beautiful oval almost surrounded by the loop of the River Wear, and overshadowed by the enormous mass of Durham's Norman cathedral. At one stage I was captain of three teams within the university at the same time, and played with each team almost every week, The university side was a most accomplished one and included players from three minor counties, one Indian state, and several very good league clubs. I honestly think it was a side that could have extended an average Cambridge or Oxford team. We even had a soccer international-to-be though we were not aware of the fact. Warren Bradley, the Manchester United and England outside-right was a fellow Hatfield man, though I knew him primarily as a hard-hitting left-handed batsman. In my last year at Durham the university side became the champion university cricket side in England outside the two major universities. The day we won the title was both a sad and a joyful occasion; on that very day I learnt I had failed my degree examinations. Later, I re-sat – and passed – my finals, but not until I had already taken up another career, professional cricket. Even when I was playing six-day-a-week cricket, I was studying, for I was determined not to abandon my father's ambitions for me. It is a little-known fact that my text-books accompanied me all the way through that victorious tour of Australia in 1954, and my favourite bedtime reading was Chaucer's *Canterbury Tales* and Wordsworth's *Prelude*.

I have many friends in the North-East as a result of

my association with Durham University. While I was at college, one of these friends invited me to play cricket in his home town of Redcar, and so it was that I came to meet my future captain in Australia, Len Hutton. Yorkshire always play several one-day matches at the beginning of the county season, and on this occasion one of them was at Redcar, against the town eleven.

Fred Trueman was playing snooker in the pub across the way when Len Hutton and Frank Lowson opened for Yorkshire. He was pretty certain his services as a batsman would not be required for quite a while. I suppose as Len Hutton took guard and saw me measure out my fifteen-yard run, he thought he was about to meet another youngster who ran faster than he bowled. For one over I tried to disabuse him of this idea. When all six balls had gone without a run being scored, he turned to the wicket-keeper and said;

'Who the hell's this?'

Years afterwards he told me I was very fast even in those youthful days, and swore that he had told Lancashire about me.

I know in my college cricket days that I was already a genuine fast bowler. It is not difficult to realise when you are too fast for the batsman; the downward swing of the blade begins too late, and the ball hits the wicket-keeper's gloves with a satisfying 'thwack'. The slip-fielders retreat a few yards every time you let an extra quick one go, and the batsman seems preternaturally pale when he takes his nervous guard.

Often I wonder whether I was not as quick in those days as I have ever been. I was not very heavily built – I weighed a mere eleven stone – but I was fresh, and filled with the tremendous zest of bowling fast. Both qualities come hard to the honest work-a-day county fast bowler. I once asked Ray Lindwall what he advised me to do about bowling fast through a full English season. His reply was direct and frank.

'Personally,' he said, 'I should bowl off-spinners!'

The natural corollary to the question 'Why did you not play for Lancashire?' is 'How did you come to play for Northamptonshire?' The answer is that Northamptonshire spotted what Lancashire did not want to see: that I could bowl fast. In the early 'fifties George Duckworth took a Commonwealth side to India and, on their return, rather than disband immediately, they played a series of Sunday exhibition games. One took place at Knypersley, and I had the chance to prove what I was worth against players of the calibre of Worrell, Livingston, and Tribe. Apparently I made an impression, for immediately after the day's hostilities Jock Livingston approached me.

'We're not supposed to poach for players,' he said, 'but if you want to play county cricket, there is a place for you at Northampton.' The idea that he was poaching was laughable, for after all, there in the pavilion was an old Lancashire player and future Old Trafford committee-man – George Duckworth – watching me play without making a sign that I should be welcome at Manchester. Jock Livingston was already playing with Northamptonshire and by the summer of 1952 I had joined him. My trial with the Midland county had been satisfactory; I had been offered terms, and my residential qualification began while I was still at university. In my first season as a county professional, I had the distinction of playing against the touring side.

The umpire for the Northamptonshire *v.* Indians match was Ken McCanlis. In later years he and I became firm friends, and I drew a great deal of amusement from hearing the umpire's eye-account of my first over for my adopted county. Most of my team-mates had never seen me bowl flat out, as this was my initiation match, and I had only been down from college a few days when I was thrust into county cricket. Indeed, I honestly believe some of the Northamptonshire players had never seen me bowl at all.

The first two balls were uneventful. The Indian batsman was Pankaj Roy and he watched them safely past the wicket outside the off-stump and into Ken Fiddling's gloves. When I marched back to my bowling mark for the third delivery, I had already made up my mind to let this one really go. Out of the corner of my eye, I saw Freddie Jakeman at first slip crouch as I tore up to the wicket. As I gathered myself for the final paroxysm of energy, I reached for the sky with my outstretched guiding left hand and tried to rap the ground behind me on the downward swing of my right arm. The ball zipped down the pitch, and moving just a little in the air, flicked the outside edge of Roy's bat. It flew straight and true, knee-high, to Freddie Jakeman, at slip. He had not time to blink an eyelid, to say nothing of touching the ball with his hand. The hollow crunch of ball on knee-cap could be heard all over the ground and Fred collapsed with a yell. After five minutes he was able to stand and the game continued, but Ken McCanlis assured me that the slip fielders took up positions five yards deeper than previously and, even as I ran up to bowl, Fred Jakeman could be seen edging still farther away from the wicket. Fortunately for the fieldsman, Pankaj Roy was caught behind the wicket off the last ball of my first over, and justice was done.

Recently a young Yorkshire player told the Press, after his return from a trial period with a southern county, that the 'Southron' folk did not take their cricket seriously enough. It reminds me of the old Yorkshire pro who, rebuking some levity in a younger player, asked him that famous rhetorical question: 'What do you think we play this game for – fun?' I recall vividly that when I first crossed the Trent to play cricket, I was particularly impressed by the game's lack of northern dourness.

Shortly after the Indian match, and during my qualification period, I played in a Northamptonshire club and ground fixture at Buckingham. I chanced to be bowling when 6.30 and the time for the radio cricket scoreboard came along. After walking the full distance back to the end of my run, I turned, expecting to see my fieldsmen straining like greyhounds in the slips. Nothing could have been further from reality. There were my fieldsmen gathered around a car-radio listening to the county cricket scores! There could have been no greater sacrilege to my northern non-conformist mind.

The qualification period, when I joined Northamptonshire, was one year. For me it was a full and happy time. I was still playing week-end games with Knypersley and my weeks were occupied with friendly games against the second elevens of other counties. There was, too, the chance to meet some of the great players and characters who used to play for Northamptonshire. One of my first minor county matches was against Huntingdonshire, when the old Northants and England bowler 'Nobby' Clark was turning out for them. He still possessed a fine high action and, though he had lost his old fire, he still had an aggressive quick bowler's outlook. Several times he was heard to mutter that twenty years ago he would have 'pinned that lucky batsman to the sightscreen.' Dennis Brookes told me, years later, that 'Nobby' did indeed bowl a fine bouncer; a ball which would sometimes move off the seam and make the terrified batsman duck the wrong way!

Not only was Ted Clark a fine bowler, he was a character of the first order. At our first meeting he told me of his tour of India with the M.C.C. team under Douglas Jardine in 1933. Most fast bowlers reap very meagre rewards on matting wickets, and most Indian pitches in the 'thirties were of this type. Nobby was no exception to the rule and his figures showed that he was having a lean tour. However his luck turned and on one occasion he scaled the dizzy heights to return six wickets for very few runs. Word reached him that his captain wanted to see him in his room after the match, and anticipating at least a few words of praise, Nobby climbed to the skipper's sanctum. He waited for a while until Jardine had finished a small job he was engrossed in, and then the English captain turned and caught sight of Ted.

'Ah, Clark,' he exclaimed, 'I just wanted to congratulate you on your fielding. It has improved a hundred per cent since the beginning of the tour!'

By 1953 my foot was on the first of the steps that led upwards to the stage of county and test cricket. The prologue had been spoken, the actors were all in their places. The curtain was about to go up on my success story!

CHAPTER FIVE

# The Black Hour of Brisbane

Looking back, it all seems like a fairy story; the sort that begins – 'Once upon a time a young man sat in a hotel lounge sipping coffee.' I was the young man drinking coffee and outside the September morning still held a breath of Autumn mildness, 1954 vintage. Sitting there in the shiny foyer of that London hotel, I paid not the slightest attention to all that was going on around me. Barely fourteen months had gone by since I was sitting in the cloistered quiet of a university examination room whose well of silence was plumbed from time to time by the clang of a single bell from the nearby cathedral. Occasionally answer books rustled and a child wailed in the flagged yard beneath the windows of the examination room, and I remember well the hot face and tingling ears which were the consequences of my mental effort and nervousness.

In those not-so-distant times I had played college cricket. Sometimes I turned out against the local grammar school and quite often there was the task of captaining the university side. My performances on the field occasionally warranted a mention in the university newspaper, but never any publicity above a local level.

Now I wondered what I was doing here. Across the lobby the bulk of George Duckworth was surrounded by the impedimenta of an M.C.C. tour – for this is what the scene meant. The different shaped bags, each daubed with the distinctive colours of the touring side, denoted that the Marylebone Cricket Club was about to send a touring side to Australasia – and I was one of the team!

Suddenly it all seemed wrong, and I was beset with a wave of doubts and questionings. Was I good – or experienced – enough to bowl against Australian Test players? I could bowl fast, but could I bowl fast enough? 'Damn it,' I said to myself, shrugging it off, 'I'll try like hell and, if I don't come off, I'll set the trip down to experience.'

The national Press had no doubts about the fast bowling prodigy who had only recently hove into sight on their inky horizon. Even through the rosiest of rose-coloured spectacles, my selection was a gamble which suffered badly by comparison with the performances of the young Yorkshire fast bowler, Fred Trueman.

All these thoughts, and more, were in my mind as the boat-train snaked slowly out of St Pancras. It crept, skirting a rough brick wall against which ashes were piled high and on which someone with an acute sense of the apt, had scrawled: 'Bring back The Ashes, M.C.C.' Behind, on the platform, the gold-braided topper of the station-master bobbed up and down like a cork. Ahead lay the monotony of a two-hour journey over the flat Essex riverside. Shortly afterwards the M.C.C. party made its way past mountains of luggage, through labyrinthine customs sheds and on to the S.S. *Orsova*. The voyage was on.

I suppose every young player's first tour must seem in later years to have been the best. I know that in my memory the first trip I made to Australia stands sharply defined and clearly the most enjoyable I ever made. My preference is partly due to the novelty of the glamour surrounding such a voyage, and partly to the success I enjoyed in those short seven months. But analyse my motives as I may, I merely accept the memories which even now crowd back on me about the trip. The sound of boys' shrill voices singing the Maori farewell song as the ship pulled away from the dockside; the sudden, hoarsely shrill, surprisingly shrill siren that drowned the Kiwi Boys' Brigade good-bye, and the necklet of lights on the evening starboard bow which I knew to be the south coast of England.

I have made many such voyages and met many friends on board since my first tour. The presence of an M.C.C. touring party on the ship adds life and enjoyment to many a passenger's trip. Friends have often confided in me how much they like travelling with the cricket team; they said it was twice as enjoyable as an ordinary cruise. Frequently, however, the Press are on hand to make capital out of the fact that the touring side undoubtedly revel in their shipboard life. There are many loose accusations about all-night parties which impair the physical condition of the side. The truth is that there are too many pressmen living in too cramped a space and too little copy to be had. In 1954 there were nearly fifty pressmen on board and quite often they had to resort to manufacturing news.

On one occasion, when the *Orsova* was passing through the Great Bitter Lakes in the Suez canal, a pressman persuaded a launch of British servicemen to come alongside to get the cricketers' autographs. They certainly received a cold welcome, for not only did the pressman get his photograph and the Tommies collect their signatures, but the passengers on the rails above tried to pass down ice-cream. By the time the boat pulled away from the *Orsova*, the deck and the occupants were smothered in ice-cream. The moral is that the Press go to great extremes to report the news.

It must be realised that, when the Australian party leaves in September, the voyage out is not only a preparation for the conflict to come, it is also a rest period from the English season just past. In '54, Alec Bedser told me how much he was looking forward to the sunny days beside the swimming-pool on the ship, and well he might, for he had just bowled twelve hundred long overs in seven short months. He was a person who deserved and needed a break from cricket, before tackling the toughest opposition in the world.

Each touring party is indoctrinated with the idea that not only do they go abroad to play cricket, but as ambassadors of England and the M.C.C. So much so that I sometimes wonder if the fact that we are spreading the gospel of cricket from the traditional home of the game prevents us from playing international cricket as hard as our opponents. Be that as it may, most touring teams are true ambassadors on board and enter into every activity aboard.

The social highlight of every voyage is the fancy-dress ball, and it is almost traditional that the cricketers should win a prize. In my experience they have always deserved one, for some of their entries have been real brainwaves. There was the Calypso Band in which most of the boys played an instrument or steel drum. When the scene had been set and the announcement made, enter fifteen coal-black figures dressed in Caribbean style who had traditionally drunk a rum-punch before their entry, all singing one of the slightly less risqué M.C.C. calypsos. All that could be seen of little Roy Swetman was the tip of his pointed hat protruding over the top of an enormous drum! It was a wonderful night, enjoyed by everyone – everyone, that is, except the cabin stewards who had to deal with towels we used to wash off the boot-polish!

One of the most original ideas for a fancy-dress costume came during our return from South Africa in 1954. The shipping line that serves South Africa names its ships after the famous castles of Great Britain: *Stirling Castle*, *Edinburgh Castle*, and *Windsor Castle*. By a strange coincidence the chief brewery in the Union produces as its main beverage, Castle Lager and, during our visit to South Africa, presented us with bright red jerseys each emblazoned with Castle Beer in large white letters. It was therefore natural that on our return voyage from South Africa the whole of the M.C.C. should attend the ship's fancy-dress ball as S.S. *Cold Castle*. We donned our jerseys, constructed a hull of cardboard, enclosed Freddie Brown in the black cylinder of the funnel, and climbed inside the shell of the ship ready to make our entrance. No detail was overlooked, even to the presence of stewards to serve drinks to the 'passengers'. Unfortunately, however, there was an hour's delay and by the time our entrance was due, we were in such a frame of mind that we thought the 'funnel' should supply smoke by setting fire to his hair!

Of the individual entries in ship's fancy-dress balls over the years, several remain indelibly stamped in my memory. Trevor Bailey's impersonation of a Teddy-boy was even better than the real thing. All that was needed to transform a Cambridge graduate into a member of the Edwardian set, was a couple of sideboards, a long jacket and drainpipe trousers! Once Colin Cowdrey, already endowed with an ample posterior, had the temerity to reinforce his natural gifts with a pillow, and enter the competition as a half-partner in the theatre booking agency of Keith Prowse. A simple device on his back told the world: 'You want the best seats. We have them!'

The traditional *pièce de résistance* on these social nights was the entry of Godfrey Evans inevitably and invariably dressed as Carmen Miranda. In my touring years I can never recollect his going to a fancy-dress ball in any other costume. The focal point of his guise was, without fail, his elaborate headpiece. Basically, the hat was nothing but a fruit basket, and its elaborations were – strangely enough – fruit; but what elaborations they were! Each time the costume was produced and worn, the pile of fruit perched precariously on Godfrey's head would become higher and higher, until at the last showing the hat was two feet high. His entrance to the ballroom was ritualistic. When the lights had been dimmed, the Master of Ceremonies would announce: 'Competitor Number 10, Mr Godfrey Evans as Carmen Miranda.' In came Godfrey in a narrow off-the-shoulder dress, his balloon bosoms bobbing up and down to the rhythm of 'Ay Ay Ay, I like you very much,' and his *chapeau* leaning first this way and then that, as he performed his interpretation of a South American rhumba. Five minutes of the Evans burlesque was always worth seeing.

Every member of the touring party used to join in the ship's fun. I remember Len Hutton and Bill Edrich, both perched on a tiny table during the ship's concert, entertaining the company with a rendering of 'Susie, Susie, sitting in the shoe-shine shop.' But the inimitable Evans more than joined in the fun; it seemed as if he personified the very word. Where two or three people gathered together in the name of enjoyment, there was Godfrey in the midst of them. Did the sports officer want a Chamberlain to help King Neptune in the crossing-the-line ceremony? Evans would volunteer; and whenever the evenings lagged and the voyage became tedious and dull, the cry would go up for Evans and his version of 'The German Band'.

This was a community mimed song led by Godfrey and, as the climax of the tune came, the leader's gestures and motions would become so involved that it seemed the Kent wicket-keeper had taken to yoga:

> '*Ich can der musica*'
> '*Auf der faderlander,*' carolled Godfrey.
> '*Vos can speiler,*'
> '*Ich can speiler,*'
> '*Aufer mine telephone.*'
> '*'Allo, 'Allo, 'Allo, 'Allo.*'

With that he would make a grab as if to answer twenty imaginary telephones on his one imaginary desk. He gave the song everything and sweat stood out on his brow, the refrain swelling as he breathed deeply with effort and exertion.

Race night came at the height of the shipboard social season. The 'horses' were of wood and were propelled down the straight course of the sports-deck by female 'jockeys' frantically winding on to a drum the cord attached to the mount. The whole atmosphere of the race-course was there, down to the presence of every imaginable official; trainers, owners, starters, and stewards. The ship's crew ran the 'tote' and the betting odds were flashed on the tote-board above the betting windows.

It was the odds which worried Godfrey: they seemed to lack glamour and imagination. In a word they were too short! So every race night as long as I can remember, 'Onest Evans', the people's bookmaker, made his appearance. Just as everyone in the dining-saloon was enjoying his first course and looking forward to a pleasant evening's sport, the main doors would open and Godfrey would come in, followed by his bookie's runner. It is an alarming experience to have 'Six-to-four-the-field,' shouted in your ear just as you raise a spoonful of soup to your mouth. This is just what happened, for Godfrey would make a grand tour of the saloon taking bets and offering advice. His dress was an extravagant caricature of what everyone expects of a bookie: his suit was a violent check, with plus-four trousers, underlined, as it were, with brown boots; a garish waistcoat hid his shirt, and around his neck was a multi-coloured cravat. A large flower adorned his button-hole, and an enormous cigar was stuck in his mouth. As a crown to the whole creation, a tiny bowler hat perched on his head. As I write these lines, I cannot help wondering how many people reading them will recognise the amusing character who disrupted their dinner with shouts of 'Get your lolly on! Six-to-four-the-field-bar-one!' and took their money for some charitable seamen's cause.

Godfrey was the same ball of fire in everything he did. Many times I played against him at squash or deck-tennis, only to be run off my feet by a man, I am ashamed to admit, nearly ten years older. Every touring team would set aside each Saturday evening for a 'get-together' or club meeting. Godfrey was always the life and soul of the party, ready to sing a song, make a proposal for the benefit of club finances, or join in any devilment. Everything he touched seemed to be charged with a dynamic force.

It was the same on the field. I have often thought the presence of Godfrey Evans behind the stumps was worth two ordinary mortals. He was more than the stumper of the side: he was the chief whip of the party. I can picture him now, as he prepared to take the ball, his blue M.C.C. cap well down over his eyes, and his gloves palm-flat on his thighs. As the bowler began his run up he squatted, legs protruding like the ungainly wings of a perched eagle, and blood-red fingers knitted and pointing to mother earth. Over the first few yards preparatory to taking the ball, he was the fastest thing I have ever seen on two human feet. Every fieldsman who chased a batsman's stroke was urged on from behind the stumps by Godfrey who stood arms akimbo and hands gripping the top of his legs. No throw, however wild, was too far or too high for him to reach. He would literally run or fling himself the length of the pitch to gather a return; but should the fieldsman's throw be really high, wide and handsome, woe betide him, for Godfrey's glare left him in no doubt as to his opinion. On the last tour of Australia Ted Dexter was often an offender in this respect, and his throw, bisecting the pitch, would fly like a rocket to the boundary for four overthrows, leaving Godfrey grovelling, still reaching for the ball and muttering imprecations.

It was sometimes difficult to live up to Godfrey's standards. He expected everyone to give to the game what he himself gave – a supercharged everything. In a Test Match, his whole heart was on the field and in his 'keeping'. It was a great feeling for a fast bowler to know that Godfrey was behind the wicket. The quick bowler, because he *is* fast, *must* put everything into his bowling and he can have no greater boost than to know that a player of the same kidney stands behind the stumps. Nothing is so disheartening as missed catches, accompanied by the knowledge that the catchers have not their whole heart in their job. Such an accusation could never be levelled at Godfrey Evans.

It is not my intention to give the impression that Godfrey is, or was, infallible. I think that he himself would be the first to admit that he has made a few costly mistakes in his time. Had he stumped Bradman at Leeds in '48, England might easily have won that Test Match. Probably, as far as technique goes, there have been 'keepers who have equalled and, in some cases, surpassed him. One might mention such revered names as Strudwick, Duckworth, Oldfield, and Tallon. But of one fact I am absolutely certain – the wicket-keeper has never lived who extracted as much from life, cricket, and his own team as Godfrey Evans of Kent and England. He will be difficult – if not impossible – to replace.

Two months after we set sail from Tilbury, our Dakota climbed steeply from Mascot airfield, circled Sydney and plunged away northwards into the tropics. The harbour and the Hawkesbury river beneath the wingtips gave way to rugged, mountainous terrain whose vegetation wore a paint-box green not normally associated with Australia. Since our arrival we had found that there was more to the country than sheep and dry open plains and deserts.

Yellow ribbons of road seemed to be the exception rather than the rule. For a while the plane quitted the coast and, at a height of seven thousand feet, passed to the landward side of Newcastle, a black smudge on the starboard horizon. Seated in the pressurised comfort of the cabin, I tried to follow the course on the map. The Dakota flew past Gloucester, over the Nowendoc river and Kangaroo flat: beneath us now a skein of streams and the smoke of a train negotiating the twisting, turning gradients of the mountain tracks. Close to MacClean and once more we were following the line of the coast. The breakers of the surf rolled white, contrasting with the deep blue of the ocean. The sands of the chain of intermarried bays afforded a yellower tint of white to the picture. Yes, there was certainly more to this country than just sheep! Mile upon mile of beaches, unending parabolas of yellow, bracketed the way northward. We were on our way to Brisbane, the scene of the first Test.

The heat and humidity were like a wall as I stepped from the aircraft. Suburban houses perched high on stilts, like H. G. Wells's monsters of *The War of the Worlds*, out of the reach of termites, well-ventilated by windows and floorboards. The bronze, overhead sun beat down on the open tramcars that rumbled up the incline of Elizabeth Street, outpacing the strollers beneath the verandah sidewalks. Most Australians wear hats by choice, but in Brisbane the hot sun makes them a necessity. The river Brisbane flows sluggishly, sepia-tinted beneath Storey Bridge, rivalling Melbourne's River Yarra for the title of the only river in the world to flow with its mud on top.

Queensland was Tyson country. The Australian poet

Banjo Patterson, wrote of one of its most famous denizens, the country's first millionaire:

*Across the Queensland Border line*
*The mobs of cattle go;*
*They travel down in sun and shine*
*On dusty stage and slow.*
*The drovers, riding slowly on*
*To let the cattle spread,*
*Will say: 'Here's one old landmark gone*
*For old man Tyson's dead'.*

Though Queensland was old man Tyson's country, it was destined not to hold any fond memories for young man Tyson.

The name of the cricket ground at Brisbane is the Woolloongabba; in the aborigine tongue the word means 'the ground of the scented wattles' It is a euphonic name for an oval which has witnessed many English cricketing disasters and defeats. In the 1950 tour England had been caught on a real Brisbane 'sticky'; a pitch on which the ball rears brutishly from a full length. It seemed that misfortune courted the M.C.C. when they played at Brisbane, and the stage was set for another catastrophe. Already the tour had a legacy of injuries and with Jim McConnon and Bob Appleyard unfit, our spin bowling strength was reduced to one player, Johnny Wardle. Worse was to follow, for on the morning of the Test Match, Godfrey Evans was down in the grip of a severe attack of 'flu.

To read the Press on the morning after that first fateful day of the Brisbane Test was to think that the English captain Len Hutton had been completely duped. He won the toss and elected to put the opposition in – always a risky course of action on Australian wickets. The general outcry in the Press led one to believe that the curator of the Woolloongabba had deliberately misled the English skipper into thinking that the wicket was as green as it had been during the preceding state match.

This was quite true. The Test wicket was as green as its immediate predecessor. It was a slab of cricket moribundity, twenty-two yards by three. In a word, it was a beautiful track, and Len Hutton was perfectly aware of the fact. The skipper's main problem had been set by the team selectors two days before the match. Limited, as they were, to one spin bowler who had only taken eight wickets on the tour to date, the committee decided to place all their confidence in the four fast bowlers who had enjoyed most success: Brian Statham, Alec Bedser, Trevor Bailey, and myself. If one discounted Denis Compton as a bowler, there was not a spinner in the side, and no advantage could be derived from bowling last on what might prove to be a crumbling wicket. The England side had no bowler capable of exploiting these conditions and the Brisbane pitch held out no promise of disintegration. Nor was there any danger of a Brisbane 'sticky dog' for the side batting last, since the wickets were to be comprehensively covered throughout the series. On the debit side, Len Hutton realised that if his fast four failed in an early break-through his team faced an enervating and morale-sapping three days in the field.

Guided by these inescapable arguments the English captain attacked as best he could with the forces at his disposal. Precedents were cold comfort to him. On the eve of the match I recalled that Jardine's team went into the Melbourne test of the 'Bodyline tour' without a spinner – and that turned out to be the sole success notched by Australia in the series.

It was Walpole who said, 'They now ring their bells, but they will soon wring their hands.' I wrung my hands after Brisbane, but it was, oh, *so* near a case of ringing the bells. What if we could have used the early life and moisture in the wicket? What if Denis Compton had not broken his hand? What if we had not missed so many catches? Oh yes, particularly, what if we had caught our catches! How true it is that catches win matches.

Observers told us later that we missed fourteen catches, none of them easy. But though one does not expect the easy catch in Test Matches, one should accept difficult and simple alike. Early snicks flew to the left and right, but never into the waiting hands of Bedser, Hutton, and Edrich in the slips. Even Trevor Bailey's usual composure was shaken when he dropped an easy chance off Arthur Morris at long-leg. He later redeemed himself by catching Neil Harvey brilliantly – but 162 runs too late! Keith Andrew, deputising for Evans behind the stumps, touched Morris's glance off Bedser. It was hardly a chance, but substitutes for Godfrey Evans must expect comparisons.

Were I a mathematician, I should remember the Brisbane Test much as I should memorise a mathematical progression. At the end of the first day, Australia had only 208 on the board and England had done well to limit their scoring; but our opportunity of dismissing them had evaporated in the hot tropic sun and there was no more help to be hoped for from the wicket. They came to 500 inexorably on the second day and the sixth century was a matter of course on the third.

After the South Australian Favell had departed with the score at 51, it was 274 runs later before the next catch was accepted. Arthur Morris edged the ball to second slip, where Colin Cowdrey engulfed it in an ample abdomen and secured it in position with his hands. The Australian vice-captain had played soundly, swinging the ball away heftily on the leg side, and punching the half-volley back past the bowler. By contrast, the innings of his partner in crime, Neil Harvey, was a blend of delicacy and power, uncertainty and deftness.

Freddie Brown once described Neil Harvey as the worst great player he had ever seen –

*When he was good he was very, very good,*
*But when he was bad he was horrid.*

At Brisbane, he glanced, drove, and cut at will. Yet occasionally he offered full-blooded shots which failed to make contact by wide margins. His composure was magnificent, and his misses never seemed to worry him, but one felt that, had such shots come from one's own bat, an edged catch must inevitably have resulted.

The major run-getters were Harvey and Morris, but Miller was Prince of Woolloongabba. This innings was the best I have ever seen from him. Three times in one over he rose to his full height and slashed my bowling against the pickets. The crowd thrilled with unsuppressed anticipation. For my part I was furious – but too tired to do much about it. A bumper after a full day in the Brisbane sun was almost too much to ask for. Mercifully Miller left, disdainfully trying to cut a Bailey half-volley and getting a thin edge on to his stumps.

Throughout the Australian innings the temperature

hovered around the century mark. The humidity was choking and as I moved back to the end of my twenty-five yard run, I looked up at the score-board. An Australian score-board can be a disheartening sight. It carries the full details of the match: the current batsmen and their scores, the dismissed batsmen – and the bowling analyses. Against each of the bowlers' names the century of runs had gone up. As I turned to move in to bowl, my leg stiffened suddenly and I found that I had cramp. The heat was such, and I had sweated so much that my body was short of salt. I left the field for several overs to swallow salt tablets and recover. Each time I left the field I had to change every item of clothing, down to my flannels. It was so hot that, after bowling half a dozen overs, even my trousers were saturated with sweat. A couple of salt tablets, a glass of beer, and I was out in the torrid sun once more, my sun hat flopping around the nape of my neck. God, my first Australian Test wicket was a long time coming! My first victim was Graeme Hole and, ironically, I did not bowl him out: I ran him out!

He glanced a ball to long-leg and, envisaging a lazy or tired pick-up and return, the batsmen embarked upon a second run. Even as they started my stride lengthened, I swooped on the ball, picked up and threw hard, a prayer on my lips that the return would be accurate. Wonder of wonders! The ball skimmed the bails and it was a mere formality to remove them with Graeme still a foot out of his crease!

I had to wait a whole day before another wicket came my way. By this time Australia were past the five hundred mark and when Richie Benaud presented Peter May with an easy catch off a mis-cued slog, he seemed to have made me a gift of his wicket. I remember I looked up at the score-board and almost wished that Richie had not thrown his wicket away. I could not make up my mind which looked the worse; nought for 160 or one for 160.

Even Ray Lindwall weighed-in with a well-made 60 and my temper became so frayed that I forgot myself and let him have a bouncer. At Sydney, Ray returned the compliment – with one important difference: he hit me! I suppose I asked for it; at least I started it.

Much water has flowed under the bridge and many victorious Test Matches have come my way since that racking in the Brisbane sun, but still it remains my blackest cricketing hour. It does one good to realise that, no matter how gifted the cricketer, or how lucky, there is a time in his career when skill and luck are of no avail, and he is reduced to the level of ordinary humanity. In the long run there is no room for the conceited player in the game: the greater his self-opinion, the greater his fall. Cricket is the greatest leveller of all.

As I sit writing of those days, impressions of my darkest hour flood back. There was a tram track which ran alongside the 'Gabba', and beyond the rails, perched on the building opposite, was an enormous blue and red sign advertising Atlantic petrol. As the days grew longer and the Australian score mounted towards the final total of 601 for eight wickets, the sign appeared to grow larger each time I ran to the bowling crease. Even as we walked off the field after the declaration, I realised we should not field again in the match.

Fatigue and demoralisation, those great enemies in hot climates, were obvious in the English batting from the very first ball bowled. In our first innings only Bailey and Cowdrey offered any spirited resistance, and their stand was brought to a most unsatisfactory conclusion. Colin was adjudged caught in the gully off Bill Johnson though, from the pavilion, the ball seemed to go off Colin's boot and not his bat. It is strange to think that on each of the occasions Colin Cowdrey has played in a Test Match at Brisbane, he has been the main actor in a miniature drama of a catch which was not a catch – at the same wicket. Four years later he was given out on the same ground, at the same wicket, caught by Lindsay Kline at short-leg, when the ball carried to the fieldsman on what seemed to be the half-volley.

The last wicket to fall in the English first innings total of 190 was Trevor Bailey's. His top score of 88 included a surprising but rewarding six. On the eve of the match, a local businessman offered £100 reward for the first six of the game, and 'The Boil', as the Aussies call him, in response to many years of heartfelt appeals from the locals, ''Ad a go,' and was a hundred pounds wealthier!

When England followed on, we fared little better than in our first innings and only topped the previous score by 67. At times it seemed that the guts of Bill Edrich and the concentration of Peter May were going to bring off the impossible, but when Brian Statham was well held in the outfield by Neil Harvey, we still needed 154 runs to make Australia bat again. The innings gave me an opportunity of noting the self-criticism which is so much a part of Peter May's batting make-up. He was leg-before-wicket to a ball from Lindwall which seemed to be missing leg-stump.

'That looked a poor decision, Peter,' I said.

'Oh, no,' replied Peter. 'It was a pretty bad shot.'

It has always been so. Peter is his own hardest task-master and harshest critic.

After the match we changed in a leisurely manner. The tension of the five preceding days was over and it was good to feel rested in mind, though uneasy in conscience. I had tried my best and it had not been good enough. At one stage it looked as if the thunderstorms, for which Brisbane is so famous, might come to our rescue, but the sixth day's sun had been just as hot and scathingly bright as its predecessors. Still, what was the point of worrying? To-morrow was another day and Sydney was another Test Match.

Street clothes were deliciously cool after the stickiness of sweat-sodden cricket shirts. An ice-cool beer slipped down wonderfully well and, with both teams drinking and joking together, the iron bath at the end of the room was soon emptied of its bottles and ice. Two hours later I stepped out once more into the evening sun, the more merciful brother of the one which had heated the after-noon's hot-plate. Across the ground little knots of specta-tors were gathered on the middle, inspecting the pitch much as they do the whole world over. The Atlantic sign was still there.

That evening, Len Hutton invited Brian Statham, Bill Edrich, Abe Waddington – the former-Yorkshire fast bowler – and me up to his room for a drink. As we sipped a glass of excellent ice-cold Australian champagne, we listened to the skipper's cricket shrewdness. He was far from disheartened by the Test for, though the margin of defeat seemed more than conclusive, England had not enjoyed the best of luck. Next time we should hold our catches and the god of luck would smile more benignly upon our cause. Less injuries and better catching and we should extend and beat Australia. Even at this early stage Len Hutton had confidence in his fast bowlers and, as Brian and I listened, we realised that the series was far from over. The real struggle had only just begun!

CHAPTER SIX

# Victory at Sydney

Every cricketer in Australia is a friend of Mr Menzies, the Australian Prime Minister, and every touring side that visits the Commonwealth plays for him at Canberra. The hundred and sixty miles of brown uplands which lay between Sydney and Canberra slid quickly beneath our plane. It was evening and an electrical storm was raging to the south and east. Sheet lightning illuminated the heights of the mountains a bare two thousand feet beneath the wingtips.

In the Australian capital, the Prime Minister gave a dinner to his team on the eve of the match against the M.C.C. His captain, Lindsay Hassett, was giving advice to the men under him, from the safety of retirement.

'Now look here,' (to Johnson, Miller, Harvey, and Benaud) 'I can't see that this fella' Tyson's as fast as you all seem to think.' He paused, then added, 'When he bounces one at me, I'll hook him out of sight.'

At this precise moment a terrific clap of thunder and a blinding flash of lightning punctuated the little Victorian's remarks. He did not pause for breath.

'There you are,' he continued, 'The Typhoon's started his run-up already!'

On the following evening, both teams gathered round the Premier's board, where they were treated, not only to an excellent meal, but also to a feast of wit. Mr Menzies told of the time he was fortunate enough to be present at the murky Nottingham Test of 1953. It was during one of his chance visits to England, which happened to coincide with the Test series. His host on this occasion was a member of the English peerage with a habit of suffixing his remarks with the exclamation 'What!' The conversation ran along these lines:

'Dreadful day, what?'

'Yes, Your Grace.'

'This confounded drizzle's spoiling the game, what?'

'Yes, Your Grace.'

'Doesn't seem to be affecting this fella' Bedser, what?'

At last Mr Menzies could stand it no longer and exclaimed: 'Not Watt, Your Grace, Menzies.'

That evening the Australian leader told us how he had always been a great admirer of Don Bradman and had watched his career with interest throughout the years. In the 'thirties he once saw Bradman score a brilliant century at Sydney. In those days, though his gifts were unmistakable, the Don's lack of orthodoxy was decried in many quarters. A New South Wales committeeman, turning to the future Prime Minister, commented that some of the Bowral boy's shots were very agricultural. Mr Menzies contented himself with the answer:

'Yes, but very fruitful.'

Only one match separated the Canberra game from the second Test at Sydney. There was just this one more chance to tune up and prepare ourselves for our revenge. Though it was only a state game, and one which was the usual anticlimax before a Test, the Victorian match was one of the most decisive in my career. It was at Melbourne that I decided to shorten my run, and it was this decision which brought me success. The shorter approach caused quite a stir, especially when it yielded six wickets in its first outing. My pace was hardly affected, but I found I could bowl with a great deal more accuracy.

Many people ask me why I changed my run, and they generally labour under the misapprehension that I had never bowled from the short distance before. But that is not so; the shorter process was not something new; it was a return to an old practice – in fact, to the run-up I used when I played league cricket.

The main reason for the reversion was the Brisbane match. At one stage of that Test I had bowled from a few paces in an effort to keep down the scoring before the arrival of the new ball. I felt that if each match was going to be played under similar climatic conditions and would result in similar exhaustion then I had better adapt my technique to meet those conditions. But this was not my sole reason for the change: the idea had been in my mind long before those five broiling days in the sun. In my very first Test Match – against Pakistan at the Oval in 1954 – Len Hutton had commented that my run was unnecessarily long. During the net practice on the day before the game, the skipper approached me and passed on his thoughts on the subject.

'Don't you ever bowl off a shorter run, Frank?' was all he asked. He had allowed the matter to rest there, but the suggestion stayed with me. Alf Gover, the former England and Surrey bowler and my mentor, also suggested that a shorter run in Australia would be a wise course. After Brisbane I was forced to agree with him.

Two days before the second Test, our overnight train

from Melbourne was approaching Sydney in fits-and-starts. The morning began for the manager with a conversation between two Australians who had apparently been celebrating the night before and were now chatting outside Mr Howard's sleeper.

'Hi Jack, are ya in good nick?'

'Jees, how crook can yer be before yer die!'

Adelaide, the genteel; Melbourne, the aristocratic; and now Sydney, the cosmopolitan. Gone were the regular line of Melbourne's blocks and intersections. Districts had their own atmosphere; Surrey Hills and Vaucluse contrasted in tone as harshly as Mayfair and Stepney; King's Cross had the aura of Soho. One looks at the map of Sydney and its environs and the names of the suburbs clustered along the hundred and fifty miles of the Harbour's foreshore trip musically off the tongue: Rushcutter's, Double, and Rose Bays: Mosman, Clontarf, Cremorne, Beauty Point, and Balmoral. The beauty of the ocean beaches are matched only by the euphony of the names: Maroubra, Coogee, Bronte, Tamarama, Bondi, Curl-Curl, Deewhy, and Narrabeen, all seem to breathe the very spirit of Australia. From the Botanical Gardens one gazed across the waters of Farm Cove and the Harbour to the shore where one knew the animals of Taronga Zoo stared back. In these urban gardens the first England *v.* Australia cricket matches in Sydney were played. Above all towered the skeleton of the Harbour Bridge, overshadowing Circular Quay, and looking Port Jackson squarely in the eye.

'What d'yer think of our Bridge?' and 'What d'yer think of our 'Arbour?' are the standard questions which mark the high degree of civic pride inherent in most

Sydneyites. Of course, too, there is always the additional, disinterested question: 'What d'yer think of our beer?'

On the eve of the match, sheet lightning illuminated Sydney and thunder rattled the windows of our Coogee hotel. I rubbed my hands as I listened to the torrential downpour and imagined the condensation that would be forming even now under the covers. Though Denis Compton's optimism about his hand was misplaced, the England side was otherwise at full-strength. Godfrey Evans was back behind the stumps and we were particularly strong in seam bowling. I visualised, with some relish, just what Alec Bedser would do to the Australian batting on a Sydney greentop.

The bombshell fell on the following morning when, a quarter of an hour before the start of the match, Len Hutton announced that Alec had been left out of the side. In a way I felt responsible for his omission. I was certain that my form in the Victorian match had led to him being dropped from an England side to meet Australia for the first time since his Test career began in 1946. I felt sorry for Alec. His current form clearly indicated that he had not fully recovered from the severe attack of shingles that had struck him down earlier in the tour. Indignation followed sorrow, for surely Alec, as a senior member of the touring side, deserved better than a public announcement of his omission in a crowded dressing-room, fifteen minutes before the start of the game! It made me all the more determined not to let him down.

Undaunted by Hutton's mistake at Brisbane, Arthur Morris, deputising for the injured Johnson as captain, won the toss and put England in to bat. Early events were to confirm him in his decision. The English openers appeared at the pavilion gate: Hutton and Bailey – an unusual and imaginative combination which led one to think back upon the number of times these two had stood individually between the Australians and victory. For 35 minutes Trevor held on, dogged and barnacle-like, sinking his fangs into Lindwall like a bulldog, until Ray drew his teeth by removing his middle stump. The sum total of Bailey's effort in terms of runs was nought.

Peter May came and went – caught at short-leg off Archer – and for a while the burden of the innings fell upon the shoulders of Hutton and Graveney. English hopes rose – but, alas, too soon. All round the ground went up the jubilant cry 'Hutton's out.' Len lightly deflected a Johnston in-swinger, only for Davidson to pick up a miraculous catch at leg-slip.

The skipper came in.

'I thought it was four runs. You can't leg-glance nowadays without someone catching you out!'

I once heard Jack Hobbs say that the main difference between opening before the war and nowadays was that, before, the leg-glance was a stroke which invariably yielded four runs; afterwards – well, look at the skipper at Sydney!

Five runs later Graveney followed his captain, caught in the slips; and, in spite of Rock of Gibraltar tactics from Cowdrey, the English batting crumbled to 99 for eight wickets. Then followed one of the most amazing cricket interludes it has been my privilege to witness. While Brian Statham presented a solid front to all-comers, Johnny Wardle sauntered down the wicket to the fast bowlers. If he connected solidly, the fieldsmen in front of the wicket were too few and far between to be of use: if his mashie shots sliced the ball away, the slip-fielders were far too close to reach the catch. Quite soon the Sydneyites were watching the quick bowlers using a Carmody field set so deep that the placing were more like baseball positions.

The score reached 154 before Wardle skied the inevitable catch to Jimmy Burke at mid-on. As if in sympathy, the heavens wept.

Only half an hour's play remained when the weather permitted a resumption. Before it had been possible to cover the wicket, quite a lot of rain had fallen, leaving the skipper with the not unreasonable hope that the pitch would be lively. Rather than risk wasting the life in the wicket and the newness of the ball, Hutton preferred to use only the bowlers he knew to be the most accurate. I was dying to get at the Aussies, but I had to watch as Brian Statham and Trevor Bailey opened the bowling. The policy paid dividends for, off the last ball of the day, Morris was caught at leg-slip from a lifter.

Saturday, the following day, was Bailey day. In seventeen overs, he yielded only 59 runs in return for four wickets – three of them the first in the order. Time and time again he brought the batsmen forward only to see his late movement beat both the bat and wickets. For once even the Hill were barracking for Bailey.

Jimmy Burke's slowness is a byword at the Sydney Cricket Ground. The Boil continually beat his bat without result and without any addition to Burke's score.

'Burkey,' shouted one wag, 'You're so like a statue, I wish I was a pigeon!'

So anxious was I to bowl that my eagerness made me waste my early spell in some wild and woolly overs. But now the gauntlet was thrown down once more. The approaches to the wicket were firmer and confidence was seeping back. The shorter run was becoming more settled and I felt the rhythm returning, mounting to a crescendo as I crashed the ball down as fast as I could. Neil Harvey being a stumbling-block for the English bowlers. The walk back to the bowling mark I always employed in two ways: in taking deep breaths to recover my wind, and in trying to think how next to attack the batsman. Now I recalled that Keith Miller occasionally used a round-arm delivery, which moved a little off the seam. Perhaps I could imitate him. My arm dropped as I flung in the round-arm delivery. It was well short, but moved back at Harvey when it pitched and, as he attempted to push it on the leg-side, it curled lazily up off the shoulder of the bat to Colin Cowdrey at gully. Victim number one! Graeme Hole was next. He had a high, flourishing back-lift which left him vulnerable to anything over average speed. A full pitched ball was on his toes before he realised it had left my hand and, though his foot was well to the line, he could only edge the delivery on to his stumps. Benaud was a palpable Statham leg-before-wicket victim, but Alan Davidson had added 20 invaluable runs before Brian executed the neat extraction of his middle stick. At the other end, Ron Archer carried Australia into the lead with a towering six, – hit to mid-wicket, which virtually depopulated one segment of the Hill for a short space of time.

The new ball arrived and Ron Archer followed the old one out of the game. 'His luck can't hold,' I thought, as I took the 'newie'. 'He can't keep edging me and get away with it.' Surely enough, he edged once too often and Len

Hutton took a brilliant catch off his bootlaces. As Ray Lindwall walked to the wicket, I was determined that there would be no repetition of his 60 at Brisbane. I would soon show him who was the boss. A man who scored 60 in the previous Test can expect a bouncer early in his innings. This one had Lindwall caught behind the wicket by the cavalier Evans. That bouncer was to cost me dear.

I paused at the end of my run and waited while the skipper left his position at short-leg and walked over to where I stood. The crowd hooted at the obvious waste of time. An entire over bowled behind Bill Johnston's rump left them in no doubt about the English policy and the barracking redoubled in intensity. The light was rapidly deteriorating and facing Lindwall in the twilight is a far from pleasant prospect. Precisely ten minutes before the scheduled close, Trevor Bailey bowled Langley with an air of affected indifference. It was timing that would have done credit to Henry Irving.

It was difficult to realise that Christmas was just around the corner. Hundreds of thousands packed the week-end beaches and the temperature seldom left the nineties. I looked on at Watson's Bay Naval base as Father Christmas, sweltering beneath his costume, arrived by car. Along Pitt, Castlereagh, and Elizabeth Streets hurried Sydneyites in search of Christmas presents, gazing into the incongruous shop-windows full of spangled hoar frost and sequined Father Christmases glittering in the hot Australian sun.

There was no festive respite for the English side as yet. The wicket had been tamed but this did not prevent the M.C.C. from losing three wickets before they finally knocked off the 74 arrears. It was left to youth – the vice-captain Peter May and his friend Colin Cowdrey – to stage a rearguard action. All through the afternoon the rival blues defied the Australian bowlers. May repeatedly rose to his full height to hit a ball of anything less than good length to the mid-wicket boundary with the precision and savagery of a well-delivered bolo punch. Cowdrey's application was so intense as to pass unnoticed, so naturally did it sit upon him. When he was finally dismissed his disappointment and the nervous reaction to his long concentration were such that he burst into tears upon reaching the dressing-room.

Peter May had just reached his century when he was bowled by Ray Lindwall. I succeeded him and very soon learnt the folly of bowling bouncers at opposing fast bowlers. The height of Ray's hand seemed to suggest a different ball, but whether it was due to the overcast morning, or a badly-placed sight screen, I shall never know. Sensing that it was a short ball I tried to duck, and turned my back on the bowler. Never again will I turn my back to a fast bowler. Something struck me a blow on the back of the skull, and I sank to the earth only dimly conscious of the ambulance men and of being helped off the field.

When I returned from being X-rayed, England were almost all out and I was in an ugly mood. Australia wanted only 223 to win and, though the consensus of opinion favoured them, I was so sore that I swore they would not win. Imagine my frustration when my efforts that day yielded no result and I left the field, knowing that on the final day Australia with eight wickets standing, needed only 151 to beat us.

The Noble stand looked high above me as I prepared to

bowl my first ball of the following morning. Reflections blinked from the giant spectacles of the Press box, crowded for the kill. At first, Burke and Harvey combined respectability with solidity. But I, too, was feeling good. My headache had almost gone and my pride was ringing from the previous day's blow. I flung every effort into my bowling, and in the second over sneaked a very fast yorker beneath Burke's bat.

There is, I believe, a psychological moment in every match when to attack with every weapon at one's disposal; the time when the opposition's confidence begins to waver and their doubts are translated visibly into strained facial expressions and hesitant movement. That time was now. Graeme Hole had barely time to lift his bat before another yorker forced its way beneath and shattered his middle and off stumps. Four Australian wickets were down for a mere 77 runs and I was feeling great. My hesitant shuffle at the end of the run was more like a bull pawing the ground, so eager was I to come to grips with the enemy. Leaning well into the run, my stride was long, and felt rhythmical; the jarring of my left foot into the wicket was sickeningly solid, and reassuringly hard.

Neil Harvey played with consummate ease while, at the other end, Benaud held on grimly. He greeted the advent of Appleyard into the attack much as its inhabitants must have welcomed the relief of Mafeking. But when their total was 106, he attempted a sweep off the slow bowler and the ball shot high from the top edge of his bat towards the regions of square-leg. There were shouts of 'Frank' and I found myself the recipient of a steepling chance. The freshening wind caught the ball and caused me to misjudge it. There was that familiar, heart-stopping moment when I realised that I had gauged it wrongly, and I completed my effort on one knee, the ball clutched in my hands three feet from my body and inches from the turf. In the dressing room, Geoffrey Howard, the manager, was doing a Dervish dance of delight.

The luncheon interval came and went all but unnoticed. Could Archer repeat his first innings performance? If he did, the match was as good as Australia's. The young Queenslander clearly decided that the solution to the crisis lay in energetic measures. For my part, I was determined that he should have nothing to hit. As I pitched short, his eyes gleamed with anticipation, and he gave himself room to indulge in his favourite square-cut. Amazingly, the seam caused the ball to break back and he had no longer any room to make his shot. The ball passed between pad and bat and as I watched with elation, rattled the top of his off stump.

All the five subsequent runs went to Alan Davidson before, with the total at 127, Brian Statham whipped one back from outside the left-hander's leg stick. Godfrey Evans had already moved over to take the ball when it flicked the inside edge of Alan's bat. From my position at deep third man, I had the impression of a bird veering in flight, the extension of an enormous glove, a heaven-shaking shout and the departure of a crest-fallen Davidson. Out of the pavilion came the man who had been the cause of my anger – Ray Lindwall. For years afterwards, his friends told him that if he had not bowled that bouncer at me, Australia might have won the series. I wondered how he felt at that precise moment. Over a hundred runs to score with only three wickets to fall, and a fast bowler he had just knocked out to face. For a moment I seriously thought of bowling him a bumper. As I moved back to bowl, I realised he would expect retaliation, and decided to keep the ball up to him. He was bowled trying to cut the fullest of half-volleys. Nine runs later Gil Langley followed him back to the pavilion – bowled by Brian Statham.

The tall, rangy figure of Bill Johnston appeared on the pavilion steps. He trailed his bat in his left hand and in his right he held a stump, the replacement for the one shattered by Statham when he bowled Langley. The crowd gave him encouragement: 'Come on Bill: remember when you and Doug Ring beat the West Indies at Melbourne.'

Australia still had 78 runs to score. Short-legs were of little use against Harvey now. Previously he had been content to execute delicate glides but now his shots put on flesh. Hefty clouts to mid-wicket chased full-blooded hooks. Many of them were uppish, but nonetheless effective. The score crept up towards the English total. Harvey farmed the bowling and left Johnston exposed for only the odd ball. Bill, for his part, stopped the straight one, and to those the now weary fast bowlers frequently put down the leg-side, he offered a peculiar brand of one-handed scoop. My run began to seem longer with each ball I bowled — and small wonder, for Brian and I had been bowling for one and a half hours. Hutton could not risk a spinner against Harvey in his present mood, but I did not seem to be able to pull the extra fast one out of the bag. Brian was flagging too, for he had been bowling into the wind. I motioned Trevor Bailey finer at long-leg and dropped one short at Neil Harvey. As expected, Neil hooked viciously to where Trevor stood. Bailey moved in, anticipating the catch, but the ball dropped over his head, and hit the pickets first bounce!

But, as a 'farmer', Neil had forgotton his rotation of crops and Bill Johnston was left high-and-dry to face an entire over from me. These two had considerably reduced the margin and the Australian deficit was now only 42 runs. Two balls Big Bill survived; the third he dispatched to the fine-leg fence with his one-handed flourish. Dear God, I thought; we have not come so close to be beaten. Come on, Frank, just one quick one!

The crowd were behind Australia to a man, cheering every shot and encouraging every boundary shot to the fence. In the midst of all this excitement a tired Brian Statham approached a weary Frank Tyson as he went back to bowl.

'Try one a little closer to his body and a little shorter, Frank.'

The next delivery was made to order. Again Bill Johnston went for his Victorian palais glide, but this time he got an edge. There was a loud snick, and as Godfrey Evans attached himself gratefully to the catch, the whole field leaped up in the air roaring out their unanimous appeal. My shout was not of triumph but of relief. We were level in the series.

Many people have asked me which I regard as my best bowling performance and I always quote my bowling at Sydney in the 1954 Test. It is not merely that I took wickets: it is that I derived more enjoyment from that success than from any other.

The Sydney Test was, without doubt, the best game of cricket in which I ever played. It had all the ingredients of a wonderful match; thrills, suspense, and skill. In the ranks of the Australians, Neil Harvey, small though he is, loomed head-and-shoulders above his team-mates. His innings of 92 contained none of the usual Harvey nuances of gaffs and genius. It was a knock great in its solidity.

I like to think of the English victory as a triumph of teamwork. I took ten wickets: Peter May scored a hundred; but these were small contributions compared with the team spirit as a whole. There were so many ifs in the game. Would England have won if Wardle, Appleyard, and Statham had not scored those valiant tail-end runs? In the whole match, Wardle only bowled four overs, yet to this very day I recall how as each Australian batsman was dismissed, he ran eagerly to the wicket and insisted on polishing the ball for the fast bowlers!

It was a magnificent game to play in. Better even than the subsequent Melbourne Test. Fortunes swayed from one side to the other and finally only 38 runs decided the issue.

That evening we were invited to a Christmas party and when we arrived, someone had drunk all the beer. Still what did it matter? We had won the second Test.

And it was Christmas!

CHAPTER SEVEN

# The Wicket at Melbourne

The Sunday following our victory we were still in Sydney. Seated beside George Duckworth on the shaking seat of a Sydney tram, I rattled past the cricket ground, passing the tall grandstand of Randwick racecourse on the right, into the suburb of Kingsford. I was blithely happy, for I was about to realise an ambition. I was going to meet my childhood hero, Lol Larwood.

In my visits to Trent Bridge, I had seen many photographs of Harold. I pictured him as a not excessively tall individual, a squat, powerfully built man, perhaps still retaining some of his former crinkly hair. I was completely wrong. Lol was slight, balding, and wore spectacles; in a word, not the man I pictured, who had been the fastest bowler in the world. If his appearance was deceptive, the trophies and photographs which adorned his walls soon gave the lie to his looks.

A few years before, the Larwood family had emigrated *en bloc* to Sydney. There was no doubting the enjoyment the Larwood girls derived from the open-air Australian life, in particular the tennis and the bathing. It gave me a twinge of satisfaction that the Aussies who only twenty-five years previously had been subjected to the body-line barrage, had accepted one of the chief executioners into their midst, and given him a home and a job. Lol was a soft-drink salesman, but his tastes ran to a harder beverage. Soon the beer was out, and reminiscences were flying thick and fast between George Duckworth and his former team-mate.

As time drew on, I asked Lol to come into town and meet some of the English team. He refused. In Australia, blame for the body-line incidents was laid at the doorstep of the person who ordered those tactics; the man in the Harlequin cap, Douglas Jardine. I think that Harold resented the fact that English official opinion placed the odium of an unpopular policy on the shoulders of the mere pawns in the game. There is no doubt that if bodyline is mentioned in England the name of Larwood or Voce springs to mind. In Australia it is the name of Jardine that is first spoken.

Harold, for his part, maintains that he has never bowled bodyline in his life. He admits to fast leg theory, and adds that if one takes time to study the records of the 1932 tour, one will find Larwood took the majority of his wickets by hitting the stumps.

Four years later, I again visited the Larwood home and again met with the same reluctance to have anything to do with the M.C.C. Again he drove me into the city and dropped me at the hotel without having a drink or meeting any of the boys. Who are we to say that he was not unfairly treated? Notoriety can be a double-edged sword.

It was good to get back to Melbourne and the comfort of the Windsor Hotel. In later years, my wedding reception was to be held in the same hotel. Across the street from where my window looked out over the incline of Bourke and Lonsdale Streets, a cinema announced its latest film in multi-coloured bulbs. The Australian poet, Adam Lindsay Gordon, on his plinth of stone, stared pondering across Spring Street. At his back lay the hollow in which Captain Cook's cottage, uprooted from its native Yorkshire soil, hid behind omnipresent gums and the windows of the Conservatory.

Melbourne welcomed us as befitted the victors of Sydney. The Australian master of the cue, Horace Lindrum, played an exhibition for us and during a visit to the South Melbourne Cricket Club, the resident parrot stupefied us with an unrivalled knowledge of Australian curses. It is said that the bird once gave a special command performance behind the Governor of Victoria's back – prompted, of course, by Lindsay Hassett.

The English team for the New Year Test was unchanged, save for the inclusion of Denis Compton, now fit, at the expense of Tom Graveney. With the resumption of Ian Johnson and Keith Miller, the only truant from the Australian side was Gil Langley who had been injured by a flying bail during a state game. His able deputy was the diminutive Victorian Len Maddocks, who had kept wicket for the Australian eleven against the M.C.C., earlier in the tour.

The big question-mark of the game was against the lasting qualities of the Melbourne wicket. In an attempt to quicken up the pitch, the couch-grass had been removed, but this not only made the wicket quicker, it also made it much more brittle. During the last Victorian game it had to be repaired. For the Test match the Melbourne Cricket Club were taking no risks and called in the outside help of Jack House, curator *par excellence*. There were cracks in the Test pitch before the match began, but this was normal. The important question was: would the pitch break up?

I always made a point of having a haircut before important matches in hot climates, since it lightens the fast bowlers' load. The barber chatted gaily about the prospects of the day's match as he ran the clippers over my head. He had not the slightest idea who I was, but it was not surprising that he was talking cricket. Everyone was talking about the match, and it was this chatter that swelled in the throats of 63,000 spectators as Ian Johnson, having lost the toss, led his side out into the field.

The English side peered anxiously from their observation window as the first ball was bowled. Watching the game from the Melbourne dressing-room was like being on the wrong side of the bars in a zoo. Spectators looked inquisitively up at the players gazing out, and their glances were equally inquisitively returned. It was all very much like the chimpanzees' tea-party.

The Press-box from its omniscient position at square-leg was already alive with the tapping of typewriter keys. It was obvious from the outset that the wicket was bone-hard, and Miller from his commanding height made several balls kick uncomfortably. In Miller's second over, the wind and the bowler moved one in at Edrich who glanced it to Lindwall at leg-slip. The fast bowler, rolling over and over, held the catch. Worse was to follow, for Peter May failed to get off the mark. A ball from Lindwall reared alarmingly, and from the shoulder of the bat the ball lobbed gently to Benaud in the gully. Cowdrey came and Hutton left, pushing at the outswinger in the Sydney and Brisbane vein, taken at first-slip by Graeme Hole.

English hopes rose with the familiar sight of Compton at

the wicket, but Denis's luck was cruelly out in these troubled times. Again Miller caused the ball to mount steeply from the cracked causeway of a wicket and, though Denis was well behind it, he could not prevent it taking him full on the glove and deflecting to Neil Harvey at gully.

At lunch Miller had returned the remarkable analysis of three for 5 in 9 overs. His doctor had ordered him not to bowl too much, because of his recent injury. One could only assume the doctor was safe in Sydney and the wayward patient beyond his control.

Bailey bulwarked the Cowdrey buttress after lunch. Colin was in great form and driving with almost lazy nonchalance, his fifty came with England's total at 90. Only a further 25 had been added when Bailey went, caught behind the stumps *via* his pads off Bill Johnston.

The Australians had slain Horatius and passed the bridge, only to find resistance where they least expected it, in the person of Godfrey Evans. Miller did not bowl in the afternoon session. His evening come-back proved that his doctor had advised him well. He was but a shadow of his pre-lunch self. The ball was now considerably softer and leapt about less alarmingly. The shine of the new ball on such wickets as Melbourne is limited to two overs, and, looking down the pitch, the bounce of each delivery was clearly marked by patches of red leather scored from the ball by the bone-hard wicket.

Godfrey was leg-before-wicket to Archer with the score at 169. Cowdrey moved to his century by turning the Queensland bowler off his body for 3 and 60,000 people cheered his valiant effort. Barely had the acclamation died down, when Wardle was bowled by an Archer break-back, and Cowdrey followed almost at once. As I stood at the bowler's wicket and watched Ian Johnson bowl to Colin, I did not dream the ball would bowl the young Kent batsman. It pitched a full two feet outside the off-stick and, on a wicket that had not turned at all, seemed to contain little threat. Colin would have nothing to do with the ball and thrust his pads at it. Alas, his foot was not to the pitch of the ball and, with my own eyes, I saw the turn take it past the back of his legs and knock down his leg-stump – a spinning distance of three feet!

The English innings closed as a matter of course with the total at 191. The Australian fast bowlers had taken eight wickets between them, but in the light of Colin's dismissal we were not disheartened, for we thought the side that had won the toss had won the match.

As I hitched up my trousers, and began to run in from the city end, the enormous crowd, inquisitive to catch a first glimpse of the new Typhoon who had struck at Sydney tensed into silence. I opened at speed, telling myself to keep the ball up to the batsman and let the vagaries of the wicket do the rest. The policy paid dividends. With the total at 15, Artie Morris shuffled characteristically across his wicket to a ball well up to him and was uncharacteristically leg-before-wicket. At the other end Favell flashed unavailingly and caused me to tear at my already thinning hair. He was a good batsman to watch, yet a player who might score two hundred in a day and still tax the memory of the onlooker to remember a single shot that combined beauty with solidity. His day was not long; he received a Statham grubber that rapped him smartly on the ankles while he obstructed the umpire's vision of the stumps. Miller had gone before, when Brian had moved a ball off the wicket, and Keith, tempted, had flicked and paid the penalty. Once Harvey hooked Bob Appleyard sweetly to the fence, a shot unrivalled in the series, but he too had to go, when Appleyard produced the ball for him; one which pitched on the leg-stump and knocked down the off. I rubbed my hands as I saw Graeme Hole coming to the wicket. A fast yorker was the ball I wanted. As I ran through the approach I had my eyes on Graeme's block hole.

One, two, three, four . . . keep the ball up there . . . The run quickened, and my strides lengthened.

Five, six, seven, eight, nine . . . grunting with effort, stretching, and over, crashing down on my left foot. It must be straight. Damn, it's too far up – it will be a full-toss. He hasn't picked his bat up yet – is it too fast for him? It's . . . bowled him!

I had bowled Graeme Hole with a full-toss!

Half the Australian side were out for 92.

Benaud played stubbornly, anticipating Appleyard's spin even where there was none. His expectations were rewarded when one turned to find his bat correctly angled, but half a second too early. Vic Wilson, fielding substitute for Denis Compton, accepted the easiest of short-leg catches. For a while the gods were with Archer and neither Brian Statham nor I could dislodge him. Nor could Archer himself find a suitable edge for Bob Appleyard's single slip fielder. Wardle finally solved the problem by bowling him with one that literally crept along the ground. The writing was on the wall, and it read perfectly clearly that the side that batted last on this wicket was in for a rough passage. Lindwall and Maddocks took the Australian total to 151, and then Lindwall failed to dig out a superlative Statham yorker.

Maddocks played solidly in his first Test, backing-up bat with body. Johnson, too, played a straight bat with a minimum amount of backlift. As the bowlers tired on an increasingly oppressive day, and the Aussie total crept ever nearer the English, both sides contented themselves with playing for the Monday morning.

In England one often sees cars by the winter roadside stopped by a frozen radiator. On Sunday, January 2, 1955, probably that very thing was happening in England; but in Australia it was quite the reverse. As the car taking Reg Simpson and I bathing sped along the Nepean highway towards the beach, the road verges were littered with cars stopped by the heat. At three that morning the temperature had topped the 93° mark and by early light the mercury registered 103°. Noon bettered this level by two degrees.

At the beach, a headwind raised plumes of spray along the crest of each breaker as it wrinkled its tiny way across the shallows. The surf was steadily backing up, and grains of sand, whipped up in the breeze, stung like hornets. There was no shelter from the sand or the heat, for shade availed nothing against the temperature. A Northerly wind was blowing from the very heart of the continent and the deserts were exhaling heat. Hotter than any Red Sea wind, the Northerly brought in its wake clouds of dust whose density blotted out the sun, giving the sky a leaden appearance. Had it rained, it would have poured red mud. Outdoors the atmosphere was as thick as the air inside a pottery kiln and the heat was inescapable.

We abandoned our bathing in despair, for there was

little enjoyment to be derived from the miniature Sahara. As we made our way back to Melbourne, we were met by a steady stream of traffic. It was the exodus, all intent on avoiding the hot city night by passing their sleeping hours on the beaches. I turned to Reg Simpson.

'I should like to see the cracks on that wicket now. They must have widened by an inch in this heat.'

The cracks on the pitch had indeed widened. The covers had been removed at nine o'clock in the morning and replaced at six in the evening. It would go hard with the side batting last on this wicket.

The two previous days play had taken place on a pitch whose hardness was like glass: so hard that spikes and studs, no matter how sharp, could not penetrate it. Several times Brian Statham had skated and fallen along his run-up, only saved from injury by his suppleness and litheness. The week-end weather suggested that Monday's wicket would be even more baked and treacherous, and the bowlers all prepared their sharpest spikes. Although the weather bureau had announced the approach of a cool change, the Melbourne furnace still functioned at full blast throughout Sunday night, and sleep was a rare treasure.

Only the wildest of optimists would have given the two remaining Australian wickets more than twenty runs on this mosaic wicket; but on the Monday morning, Brian Statham did not slip as he ran up to the wicket. His approach was sure-footed and his spikes sank easily into the ground. The cracks on the playing-area had not become wider; they had closed up! From the height of the members stand, black patches, not previously apparent, were visible on the wicket and its surrounds. The wicket was soft! It had been watered.

It took the new ball to break the partnership of Maddocks and Johnson, for the pitch was better than it had been on the first morning. Bailey was welcomed at the bowling crease by three robust Johnsonian fours which would have done credit to the great Doctor himself. Even Bill Johnston reached double figures, before Statham uprooted his off-stick, leaving him stranded in the very midst of his intended aggression.

How had the wicket become damp? This was the main topic of conversation for many a long day after the match had been decided. It was also the subject discussed by an investigating committee appointed by the Melbourne Cricket Club. Finally it was announced that the moisture had been due to heavy condensation under the covers during the night! It must have been a heavy dew, when the temperature never fell beneath 93°. Many of the newspaper reports hedged on the issue, but Percy Beames, a local correspondent, came out into the open and declared that the wicket had been damped down. Beames was an ex-captain of Victoria and a person with a reasonable amount of ready access to reliable sources of information. If one puts oneself in Jack House's shoes on that black Sunday, it must have seemed logical to water the wicket. He had been brought in to prepare the Test wicket, expressly to prevent the recurrence of the crumbling wicket of the Victorian game. Had he not acted there can be little doubt there would have been hardly any wicket left on the Monday.

The unexpected resistance of the last two Australian batsmen left England with a first innings deficit of 40 and it was precisely as they overhauled this debit that they lost their first wicket. The wicket was responding more and more to spin and the ball with which Bill Johnston claimed Edrich's wicket had turned sharply. Then Ron Archer bowled an inswinger which left Len Hutton straddling the wicket, his feet well outside the line of his sticks, but the ball had caught him in front, and the umpire's finger was up.

The skipper walked wearily in and slumped rather than sat on the dressing-room bench. For an hour he sat motionless, his head in his hands, without even bothering to take off his pads. I heard later he had not wanted to play in this Test as he thought himself unfit. It was only the opinion of the senior players and George Duckworth that forced him to play. There was no doubt he was beginning to feel the strain of the round of speeches, receptions and functions, which make the job of running a cricket team doubly difficult on a long and strenuous tour. His were the days when there was only one manager to help him out and I certainly did not envy him his job.

Cowdrey had only scored 7, when, dropping the ball defensively at his feet, he lost all interest in it. Peter May, batting at the other end, shouted a warning, but it came too late, and the ball spun slowly back on to the stumps, toppling a bail. A bruised thumb was not enough to keep Compton from the fray and at the close he and May had taken the total to 159 for three.

Of the three wickets which had fallen to quick bowlers on Monday, two fell to Brian Statham. Only Archer of the Australian quickies claimed a victim. By comparison, 13 of the 18 wickets which fell on the Friday and Saturday had gone to the fast bowlers. The moral is obvious: watered wickets and fast bowlers do not mix.

When the English vice-captain was bowled the

following morning by a Johnston spinner, after only adding 4 to his overnight score, it was immediately obvious the wicket was taking more spin. Twelve runs later Compton was caught behind on the leg-side by Maddocks, but Trevor Bailey remained lodged like a thorn in the Australian's side. Evans went to the new ball immediately after the luncheon interval, but not before he had bustled his way to a quick 20 runs. In dismissing Godfrey, Australia jumped from the frying-pan into the fire, for now they were treated to the Wardle brand of aggression. Four times in one over he hit Big Bill Johnston to the ringside, and he greeted Ian Johnson by placing a ponderous right foot down the wicket and sweeping him to the square-leg fence. The scythe shot reaped a rich harvest, and the Yorkshireman had added 38 in quick time before he struck early at a straight, flighted off-spinner, and was bowled by Ian Johnson. Bailey barnacled for some time, but wickets fell regularly at the other end and the English innings closed at 279.

The stage is set for the final act. Australia want just under 200 in the fourth and final knock; already the cracks are beginning to reopen and the wicket is less reliable. Can Australia score the runs? I was confident in my own mind that they could not.

As we took the field, we were joined by a spectator, who made his way round the whole field in a series of kangaroo-like hops while we watched with Anglo-Saxon detachment. The two white-helmeted policemen who were in hot pursuit finally captured him and led him off. I later learnt that he was a regular performer during the football season.

Each little detail crowds back on me from the past, for

this was destined to be a great innings for me. The game restarted, and for a while Favell went on his own gay way. I was trying so hard that it hurt. Every last ounce of speed was being called out. Morris was batting more phlegmatically, as if he sensed that this might be his last Test opportunity to 'come good.' When the Australian score had reached 23, I banged one down on the line of Arthur's leg-stump and the left-hander, shuffling across his wicket, fended the ball too strongly off the line of his pads. It popped up towards Colin Cowdrey at very square silly mid-on, and I held my forehead in anguish as I felt that the ball would not reach the fieldsman. But no, Colin flung himself forward to take the catch in his right hand, inches from the turf, and my anguish became jubilation. First blood to England. Miller should have been the next batsman, but instead Benaud succeeded his vice-captain at the wicket. Miller was being kept back for the effort of the morrow. The light was still excellent in spite of the late hour, and the sun was very bright. Hutton brought on Appleyard, bowling from the Richmond end, and Favell overreached his aggression at last. He stepped out to drive the slow bowler, but only succeeded in making a half-volley into a yorker. It hit the top of the middle stick. Harvey and Benaud continued sedately until half-past five, when Australia needed 165 to win the game with eight wickets standing. The match was poised for the following day.

January 5 was a red-letter day for me. Let me reproduce the cryptic entry in my diary:

'Perhaps the luckiest and certainly the happiest day of my life. I bowled out Australia before lunch!'

This was the day I had dreamed of, the fulfilment of

my ambition to go out on to the field and to bowl out the Australian batsmen just as quickly as they came in.

Sixty thousand people saw us take the field, and most of them, chatting amongst themselves, were agreed that 165 was not beyond the powers of the remaining eight wickets. They little thought of the surprises the day had in store, and, anticipating a full day's play, they had brought picnic lunches to the match. By twenty minutes past one, I had bowled out the Aussies and the game was over. The 60,000 lunches were all wasted.

I took the ball, gave it a vigorous rub and turned to take the first over from the Richmond end. It was the first time I had bowled from this wicket; the ground sloped up to the city end, and the wind was slightly in my face. Even from the end of my shorter run, the umpire seemed to be miles away, but I told myself that this was no time for worrying about small details. It was the moment for action. Slowly I moved into my run, and gradually as ball succeeded ball the pace of my first over increased. The seventh ball pitched on Harvey's legs and the left-hander shaped as if to leg-glide it. He had reckoned without Godfrey Evans. The stumper's feet twinkled over the first two yards before he launched himself to cover the remaining distance in the air and clutch the deflection to his body like a long-lost brother. At the end of my follow through, I could scarcely believe my eyes. It did not seem possible that Godfrey could have caught it; but the proof lay in the evidence of Neil making his slow way back to the pavilion.

If ever there was a turning-point in a match this was it. Before, it had seemed possible that we could bowl out the Aussies. After that catch, and the heart it put into the whole side, I never doubted for one moment that we *should* bowl them out.

At the other end Brian Statham had Miller in trouble as soon as he came in, and it was only with difficulty that he kept out a 'creeper'. Runs came slowly: only 10 from the first four overs. Bad balls were few and far between, and Richie Benaud, a naturally aggressive bat, was dying to get on with the game.

The first ball of my third over was exactly what he had been waiting for: well short of a length and outside the off-stump. It was a rank bad ball, and only bettered by an even worse shot. Richie went for the hook, only to find that the ball was too wide of the off-stick, and his wild swing merely succeeded in deflecting the ball via the bottom edge of the bat on to the middle and leg stumps. It was the stroke of a man relieved to find a ball he could hit, who then never even watched the ball or kept his head down. For my part I accepted my luck with incredulity. This was really my day.

Hole scored a single off the third ball he received and this brought Miller face-to-face with me. I have always been in awe of Keith. He has always impressed me as a complete man; charming, adventurous, and accomplished. I have feared him on the cricket field because he was one of the few men in the world who could turn the tide of a game in the space of a few overs with either bat or ball. Being a fast bowler, this has given me cause to hate him more than most players when he takes up the bat. At Melbourne on this wonderful day I was determined that Keith should have no scope for his batting talents. Trudging back to the end of my run, I summoned up the sinews to hurl him down a real thunderbolt. Scuffling and pawing the earth, I measured my distance to the wicket, found my stride and moved off, dipping my knees at first, only to rise to my full height as I delivered. My left hand balanced the sky like a tray, and my right arm described an arc, hesitant at first, but full as it gained momentum. My left leg crashed down and my body catapulted the ball down, following up, airborne and crouching. It was, without doubt, the fastest ball I ever bowled, and reared from the line of the off-stick. Keith's defensive prod failed to reach the pitch and the leap of the ball caught the shoulder of the bat. From where I stood, the catch seemed to be soaring over the slips, but at the last minute the skipper thrust up a hopeful hand. Smack! The ball hit flesh and I clutched at the sky as the catch was pushed upwards. By Hutton's side, compatriot slip Bill Edrich was on his toes with anxiety and as the ball came down behind the English captain's back, Bill dived to get his hands beneath it. Miller had gone and half the Australians were out for 87!

For a while Hole and Archer held us up. Short-pitched balls and bouncers did not trouble Graeme, and Archer was soon indulging in his favourite square-cut. One swashbuckling boundary hit the pickets at point and bounced half-way back to where I waited at the bowling crease. Australia were only three short of the century when Hole fell to Brian Statham. He edged a ball which moved slightly off the wicket and Evans took the catch gratefully.

Maddocks came and went in quick time. The very first ball I bowled to him was a yorker, and because he was on the back foot, anticipating a short-pitched delivery, he could do little but come down very hard on it. He seemed mesmerised by the ball, and both he and I watched breathless and tense as it spun from outside the off-stick, slowly, ever so slowly, on to his wickets. There were only three more wickets to fall! Two balls later I trapped Lindwall, again expecting a short ball, and moving into his wicket to be leg-before to one well up to him.

I was bowling in a daze. This was not happening to me. It was as if I were watching another bowler. Never before had I bowled like this, I was making the ball swing, in Australia! The ball which had dismissed Ray Lindwall was an outswinger which the fast bowler had tried to force away on the leg-side. I collected my thoughts and came back to the job in hand. There were only two more men to deal with. The Australian total stood at 98 for eight wickets. Their cause was, at first glance, hopeless.

Archer could make nothing of Brian Statham, but luck was not with the Lancashire bowler. Throughout this memorable Wednesday morning he had toiled without reward, but for the wicket of Hole. The batsmen played repeatedly at him but without edging the ball. Then Fortune smiled briefly on him. A Statham yorker hit Archer on the toes, skittling the Queenslander from his feet. Another yorker found its mark; 110 for nine! One run later, it was all over. Bill Johnston took a single and faced up as I made my way back to my mark for the fifty-first time that morning. I was tired but what did that matter! With victory so close, I could bowl for another hour-and-a-half. Just one more ball, Frank, one more and we are home and dry!

To a ball going away from him, Big Bill proffered a bodyless bat. As the ball left the edge and climbed steadily towards the stand where Mr Menzies was sitting, Godfrey snapped up his third catch of the morning. It was all over and my body sagged with relief. Suddenly I was very, very, weary – but also very, very happy.

The third Test was ours! The crowd surged over the fence and the players hung back waiting to applaud the bowlers as they entered the pavilion. I paused, waited for Brian Statham, put my arm around his shoulder and we passed into the dressing-room together. It was not a sentimental gesture, even less a mark of sympathy for a morning's atrocious luck. It was my way of saying thanks.

Fast bowlers always hunt in pairs and only a fellow-bowler can appreciate what it means to have the support of Brian at the other end. A batsman facing two really fast bowlers quickly realises it requires a great deal of concentration, application and guts. There is a respite when a side has only one quickie. With a fast bowler at each end, there is no escape: no running to the other end. I had taken seven for 27, but it might easily have been Brian who returned the figures. For my part, I prefer to say that we took nine wickets between us.

Brian Statham is not the flamboyant character one normally associates with the title fast bowler. He is one of the least spectacular, least acclaimed, and one of the best fast bowlers of our time. In my years of cricket I have never met a person, who, with an ogre's part to play, has been better liked and loved. He is the prototype of the gentle fast bowler, whose interests are solely his family, sleep, and a glass of beer – in that order. He is essentially a team man, and a bowler who, when the personal success was going my way in 1954 was the first to encourage me and keep me going.

Though he is endowed with terrific powers of determination, it is almost impossible to rouse the fast bowler's anger in Brian. On one occasion, when the opposition's fast bowler was giving his team-mates a particularly painful time, they urged Brian to take counter-measures when the offender came in to bat.

'No,' said Brian, 'I won't bowl him a bouncer. I'll just knock his dollies over.'

His bouncer is a strangulation effort which continually bores in at the batsman, and makes evasion very difficult. It is strange that Brian is so fast, for he is not heavily built, nor is his action a classical one. Yet I should rate his pace as above that of Fred Trueman. The accent of his bowling is not on body and weight, but on smoothness. He is double-jointed in the shoulders and removes his sweater before bowling, by grasping it at the hem at the back and pulling it up over his shoulders! So smooth is Brian's run to the wicket that it earned him the nickname of the Greyhound; but the Greyhound goes under another name – George. When I asked him why people called him George he said it was because he himself liked being called George. It was irrefutable logic.

If there has ever been a more accurate bowler than Statham, I have yet to see him. Godfrey Evans used to say that he could invariably tell when Brian was not feeling well. If one ball of the first over pitched off the line of the sticks, all was not well. At Mount Gambier, the Greyhound returned the remarkable analysis in a country eleven game of six wickets for 2 runs. At one stage he had taken six for 0.

Swing was never one of Brian's main weapons, though given a heavy atmosphere he could move the ball appreciably. His principal asset was his ability to seam the ball off the wicket, and more than any other bowler I have ever seen, he could control this movement. George Gunn the elder once showed me the method F. R. Foster passed on to him for bowling the break-back. His grip on the ball was almost identical to that used by Brian Statham.

It is a pleasure to play cricket with the Greyhound, for though facing his bowling is a terrifying experience, it is at the same time a reassuring one. His run-up, action, and the shock of bat meeting ball leave no doubt as to his pace, but never at any moment is there the fear that the ball will not be on the wicket. In the field he is a human catapult whose throw has left many batsmen stranded and far from home. His batting consists of three shots: the prop; the draw-back slash to cover; and the cross-batted slog. Ambition has never taken him beyond this mighty triumvirate. The reign of George the Gentle has spanned ten years of Test cricket. There can be no greater praise for a genuine fast bowler.

After the Melbourne victory, George forgot himself to such an extent that he forsook his normal beverage of beer in favour of champagne: a drink he regarded as 'soda pop.' Mr Menzies came down from his box to congratulate the English captain, while outside the crowd shouted for the players. I sat in the corner accepting congratulations, a glass of champagne in my hand, still not fully aware of what had happened. My head was spinning from a mixture of excitement and wine, as in my imagination I relived the game sweatily.

What would have happened if Australia had won the toss and England had batted last on that wicket? There can be little doubt that Australia would have won and there would have been a first-class row about the watering of the wicket. If the wicket had worsened uniformly, the side taking strike last would have struggled to make 50.

In reality there were two starts to the game; one before the watering and one afterwards. It was lucky for us that we had won the toss on both occasions.

Many paper clippings were sent to me from New Zealand. Most were of a cartoon that showed a cricket team peering round the corner of a pavilion, hosepipe in hand, as a slightly balding player approached, a ball in his. The caption read:

'Never mind the wicket, let's fix this bloke.'

Once more the tension and the interest of another Test Match was over; a game I shall always remember ball by ball. I hung on to the day as if reluctant it should ever end. Even a scheduled New Year broadcast was forgotten and, instead of speaking to England, I went to the cinema!

CHAPTER EIGHT

# Triumph at Adelaide

The Christmas rush was over. Two Test Matches in two weeks had been hard going and three weeks of up-country matches, hospitality and food had been just the medicine the doctor ordered. Now the convalescence was over, and we were saying good-bye to Mount Gambier and what appeared to be its entire population. The 'Mount' had just become a city by virtue of acquiring its ten thousandth inhabitant, and it seemed that not a single citizen was missing from the crowd that came to the station to wish us good luck in the Test Match that was just around the corner. Even the Girls' Brigade Pipe Band turned out to wish us 'bon voyage'.

The overnight train journey to Adelaide left us hot and sticky. Sleep had been impossible, for South Australia was in the merciless grip of a heat wave. The state capital was boiling. There had been a week of century temperatures, and we were relieved to reach our seaside hotel, overlooking the foreshore of the suburb of Glenelg. The sea breezes were balm to our souls after a day in the brick oven of the city. Adelaide conjured up visions of the English city of Worcester. Its cleanliness was astounding; the city blocks and white buildings breathed spaciousness. Even the name of its founder, Colonel Light, suggested airiness.

From the cricket ground I looked up to the squat lines

of the Mount Lofty ranges, which sandwiched the city firmly against the coast. St Peter's cathedral peered over the score-board, as though casting a spiritual eye on the drinkers in the bar beneath. At the gates of the Oval, the river Torrens flowed gently along the length of War Memorial Drive and its surrounding parkland.

There was no escaping the heat and the mosquitoes, and when M.C.C. beat South Australia in the state game by an innings and 143 runs, I wondered whether it would prove a Pyrrhic victory. As much as possible, we tried to keep our key men fresh, and hoped to win the toss, so that we could field when the weather cooled.

The English side remained unchanged from the victorious Melbourne combination, but the Australian selection was, to say the least, erratic. Arthur Morris had been omitted from the original twelve, but was re-introduced when Ray Lindwall injured himself in a state game. When the great day dawned, Arthur played, and Les Favell, who had been in the original side, was left out! The selectors certainly did not endear themselves to the South Australian public, particularly when they also dropped the now fit Gil Langley. I remember the special cheer Gil got when he walked into the ground just to watch the game.

The Adelaide Oval was crammed to its capacity of 35,000 as the deciding game began. Though it was not a large crowd, it was, like most Australian gatherings, very noisy. On our last visit the crowd had completely halted the state game by insisting on listening to the Melbourne Cup on thousands of portable radios.

If I were to draw a distinction between an Australian and an English crowd it would be that an English spectator goes to a match in the forlorn hope of being entertained;

the Aussie goes with the firm intention that no matter what the players do about it, he is determined to enjoy himself.

This explanation accounts for the individual who was watching Neil Harvey bat in the Victorian game. Neil was having a particularly torrid time and played and missed repeatedly. It was interesting cricket, but it could hardly be called entertaining, and finally the chap in the shirt sleeves jumped to his feet and addressed me;

'Oi you,' he said, 'Why don't you bowl him down a piano, perhaps he can play that!'

The Adelaide wicket was a notorious featherbed, and the side batting first could expect to keep the opposition in the field and in the sun for three days. It was an important toss to win. Ian Johnson was the lucky captain, and we his unfortunate victims. We remembered how Alec Bedser suffered sunstroke on this Oval in 1946 and had to be led off the field and put fully clothed under a cold shower. As Len Hutton led us out the thermometer had already registered 101° although it was only eleven in the morning. Colin McDonald, the Victorian, was the newcomer to the opening partnership and he and Arthur Morris put on 59 before they were separated. Somehow – I still cannot explain how I did it – I managed to get a ball above stump high. It flicked Arthur Morris's glove and Australia's best opening stand of the series had ended. The heat was beginning to tell, and although I wore a floppy hat to protect me from the sun, I felt far from the fastest bowler in the world. It was certainly not the climate for quick bowlers. McDonald came to our assistance by losing patience and giving May an easy catch off Appleyard, when his own tally was 48. Jimmy Burke soon followed, caught in the leg-trap, and Harvey was neatly taken at slip during a very good Bailey spell. In all, England were happy to have contained Australia to a mere 161 for four on the first day, and more than happy to get off the field.

Already the wicket showed promise of turn and Appleyard caused a further Australian collapse on the following day when he rid us of Benaud and Miller. There is no doubt that the Aussies would not have seen 250, had it not been for Len Maddocks. He had not been a popular choice for this game, because Gil Langley was fit and the Adelaide Oval was his home ground, but Maddocks's 69 revived his popularity.

With Australia all out for 323, England made their best start of the series to date. Len Hutton and Bill Edrich were soon going great guns and put on 60. When his own score was 80, the skipper was out in a most extraordinary way, hooking a ball hard to Davidson at short-leg. Alan turned his back on the ball, shying away from possible injury, but his evasion tactics were useless; the ball hit him squarely in the middle of the back and bounced into his outstretched hands! It was just the skipper's luck to have this happen when a century was almost within his grasp. He and Colin Cowdrey had never looked in trouble against the turning ball. Colin scored 79 and with Compton's 44 the next highest score, England aggregated 341 – a lead of 18.

When Australia batted a second time everyone expected Len Hutton would pound the openers' defences for at least an hour with his quick bowling; but no, the English skipper shrewdly only gave Brian Statham two overs before introducing Bob Appleyard into the firing line. It was a stroke of tactical genius, and the off-spinner removed both the left-handers Morris and Harvey. Jimmy Burke was his third victim and at close of play the Yorkshire bowler had taken three wickets for a personal cost of 13 runs. It was now obvious that the pitch was turning quite sharply and the English batsmen were not looking forward to taking strike last.

Next morning, after Brian Statham and I had returned from our morning run along the Glenelg beach, I lay on my bed, eating breakfast and reading the morning papers. Every paper, down to the last drop of ink, confidently stated that Appleyard was the danger man to Australia's hopes and that he would be the player to watch. It is ironic to think how right they were. Bob never bowled another ball in the match! Brian Statham removed McDonald, Miller and Maddocks in his first three overs, and I accounted for Benaud, Archer and Johnston.

How well I remember that morning! It was boiling hot once more, and yet after an hour's bowling Len Hutton gave no indication that Brian and I were to be rested. It was a paradoxical piece of captaincy that a skipper who had given his fast bowlers only a taste of the new ball on a turning wicket, should persevere with them when the ball was older and the wicket still turning. In the final analysis it was a great example of thoughtful cricket leadership. This final Australian innings could be the last lap before the winning post was passed and the Ashes were won. Since Brian and I had established a psychological advantage over the Aussie batsmen in previous Test Matches, and even now were taking wickets, Hutton pressed home his advantage and drove his fast bowlers almost to breaking point. On a morning when the temperature never fell below 90°, and even to walk about was hot work, Brian and I bowled unchanged for the whole of the one-and-a-half hours before lunch!

The last quarter of an hour dragged interminably and I was reminded of the Keatsian line:

'My heart aches and a drowsy numbness pains my sense.'

Somewhere along the way I had strained my groin and towards the end of the morning I felt I could continue no longer. Brian Statham was fielding at mid-off and I told him how I felt.

'Come on, just another few overs. We've only one wicket to go,' he replied.

So it was that over succeeded over and the morning came to a merciful end. Fortunately for me, Wardle had Alan Davidson out in his first over after lunch and Australia were all out. Had it been left to me, I doubt whether I could have summoned up enough energy to have appealed.

It had been a wonderful morning for England and a reversal for the Jeremiahs of the popular tabloids. The fast bowlers had done it again and we only needed 94 to win the match, the series and the Ashes.

Judging from the way we set about scoring the runs, it hardly seemed likely we were going to achieve our goal. Only 3 runs were on the cathedral-shadowed score-board when the mighty Miller bowled Edrich and followed this by having the English captain taken in the slips.

Len Hutton was in despair. This was perhaps the very nadir of his tour; a moment which although it was his darkest hour was so close to his greatest and to the winning of a tour in Australia. Five months of fibrositis, responsibility, worry and travel had worn through even a Yorkshire hide. He paced the dressing-room, unable to settle or sit down until the match had been won.

'It's Miller,' he said, 'The so-and-so's beaten us again: he's beaten us again.'

He was inconsolable. Denis Compton was livid. He grabbed his bat and marched down the pavilion steps, with the words:

'I'll show you who has beaten us.'

But Hutton was very nearly right. Miller was so close to breaking through the English batting that it was not comfortable, especially for the tail-end batsmen. He disposed of Colin Cowdrey in the same way as his captain and then caught Peter May in the covers. Even from the middle Peter's dismissal must have seemed dubious, but from the pickets this was the catch that never was. It clearly bounced out of Miller's hand at cover and hit the ground. Miller himself admitted that he had grassed the chance, but added that he thought he had held the ball long enough for it to have been a catch. The doubt which surrounded the dismissal was only heightened by Miller's body which surrounded the ball as it touched the floor. Neither the umpire nor Peter May could tell whether it was a catch. Peter looked at Keith. He nodded, and Peter walked. England had only 50 runs on the board.

But if Mighty Miller had decided views about the game, so had Bailey and Compton. Denis cut and swept while Bailey blocked. I am sure that if Miller's body is opened after his death, Bailey will be found graven on his heart. Trevor defied all attacks until the English total was within 4 of the Australian, when he was out, sweeping Bill Johnston. Cocksure, aggressive and confident, Godfrey Evans walked perkily, arms akimbo, to the wicket, took guard and dispatched the ball to the mid-wicket boundary. He departed crowd-chased, waving his bat aloft, and

England had won the Ashes in Australia for the first time since 1932.

What a night of celebration that was! I wish I could be truthful and tell what happened. If I am truthful, however, I must say I cannot remember what happened. I only recall entering the hotel late at night and finding Bill Edrich climbing a pillar in the foyer to win a bet. It must have been a short climb for him – he was already on top of the world!

Why did England win the series? Looking back from the eminence of the present, I can afford to be objective and state that, as results proved, we were the better side. More than being the better one, we were a side in the true meaning of the word. There were no distinctions between amateur and professional; we were cricketers who played together. Under such circumstances it is easy to tour and be a real team.

I recall one particular instance at the beginning of the tour that reflected the spirit of the touring party. One day I, the most junior member of the side, saw the mighty Denis Compton going up the hotel stairs to his room.

'Bring me a handkerchief down from my room Denis,' I shouted. The fact that he brought me a handkerchief, was more than a major victory for comradeship; it was a miracle he remembered!

The '54 side was a good blend of youth and experience; youth to bear the brunt of the bowling in roasting temperatures, and experience to guide the team and shoulder the batting responsibilities. The batsmen were more than lucky to have seasoned young men like May, and successful young batsmen like Cowdrey to strengthen their standing. At the helm was a man whose captaincy was often criticised and never understood.

I suppose Len Hutton was a difficult man to come close to and understand. I remember Keith Andrew's puzzlement when he approached the skipper for permission to play golf during a match.

'Eh lad,' said Len, 'When I was your age, I used to eat, drink and sleep cricket.'

Keith gave him a very old-fashioned look and said; 'Well, if you spent all that time watching cricket, how did your handicap reach eight?'

Len laughed and told him to play golf.

Hutton was an introvert, but one who knew his cricket. He is the only man I have ever met who has persuaded the umpires that the teams should leave the field for bad light because his fielding side could not see the ball! The incident occurred during a New South Wales game when M.C.C. were in the process of losing the match. Bobby Simpson had scored 98 and his partner was Jimmy de Courcy. The batsmen were naturally reluctant to leave the field, and remained on the pitch after the fielding side had left. It was amusing to see two batsmen facing a large crowd and quite alone. Bobby was so annoyed by the whole incident that when the light improved and the match continued, he swung wildly at the first delivery and was stumped when his personal tally was still two short of the elusive hundred.

I have good reason to know that Len Hutton was a shrewd judge of cricket, its players and situations. During the test match at Auckland in the New Zealand tour of '55, the first innings' totals were almost level when I went to the wicket with only two weak English wickets remaining. A hand fell on my shoulder as I walked out of the dressing room. It was the skipper.

'If you can get a few, Frank, we will not have to bat again.'

Well, I scored a few and the English score topped the New Zealand total by 60 – and in the second innings, the Kiwis scored 26! Len Hutton had been right; we did not have to bat again.

Many people criticise him because he overbowled his fast bowlers in his successful tour of Australia. He certainly used Brian and I a great deal, and probably it did not make for brighter cricket; but his reasons were sound. He knew full well that the English fast bowlers had established a psychological advantage over the Australian batsmen and he determined to keep his superiority even if he brought his youngsters to the edge of exhaustion. He was England's first professional captain, and one moved about in the field in the assurance that he knew what he was about. He was a player and a captain who worked at his game, and his field settings were workmanlike. Most important of all was that as a professional he was one of us. His decisions were not those of a superior being who moved in planes beyond the ken of mortal professionals; they were the combined wisdom of his senior players.

Under Len Hutton, I achieved my greatest hour, and it is this that probably colours my opinion and prejudices me in his favour. I shall never forget that under his wing I changed from a potentially dangerous fast bowler with an excessively long run to a Test Match player feared and respected by the Australians. Looking back, I have no doubt that the three years subsequent to the Australian tour were my greatest period. A stripling of twelve stone when I arrived in the antipodes, I returned, thanks to Australia's steaks and oysters, a fighting thirteen-and-a-half stone. I was fitter than at any other time in my life. My opinion as to whether my pace increased is somewhat hesitant, for, not being the batsmen who faced my bowling, I quibble at passing judgment. But I have no doubt that, when I set foot once more in England, I was a far better cricketer. Economy had not been one of my crowning assets, yet, in the course of the tour, I could feel my action becoming more compact and my run less exhausting. I stepped off the hottest cricket field less embarrassed by fatigue than of yore. My accuracy was a hundred per cent better, and batsmen could no longer let half my deliveries go without playing a shot. I was far from perfect, but I flatter myself that I was quite an unpleasant proposition for any batsman. Would that it could have lasted!

CHAPTER NINE

# Featherbeds and Turnstiles

I touched the air-hostess's sleeve as she passed down the darkened aisle of the transatlantic airliner.

'How long to London airport, miss?' I asked.

'About twenty minutes, sir.'

Only twenty minutes more and we should be home after seven months of cricket! My stomach muscles tensed with excitement and my head spun with channel fever. By my side Trevor Bailey snored gently, obviously feeling the effects of our two nights in New York. Behind us lay a week in America: nights in Greenwich village, visits to the theatre and Princeton University, the cable-cars of San Francisco, and Honolulu's Waikiki beach. My memory reached even further back and retrieved the dusty recollection of a Test series that seemed to have taken place ages ago.

Before us lay the brou-ha-ha of welcome which is the lot of returning victorious teams: official welcomes, Pressmen, bright lights, cameras and television interviews – the whole gamut of welcome which says hail the conquering heroes.

Yet it only seemed like yesterday that I was strolling into the Northamptonshire dressing-room to play my first match against the Australians. That sunny June day in 1953, after a full year's residence in the county, I was going to begin my full-time cricket career. I was fixedly determined to do well, for only two days before they had told me I had failed my final examinations, and I intended to carve out another career for myself.

Now I was the most acclaimed fast bowler in the world. Was it possible that all this had happened in two short years?

I wonder if Buddy Oldfield knew this would happen, when he first saw me. He was, I remember, the first person I saw on that eventful day two years before. He was a small dark man, continually blinking like an owl in broad daylight. The former Lancashire player was sitting on a bench opposite the door, a bat between his knees, smoking a cigarette.

He looked nervous and he was; so nervous, I learnt in later years that he could never bring himself to face breakfast before a match. It all goes to show that even the most seasoned of veterans feel those butterflies in the stomach before taking strike.

The memory of my first match against the Aussies will remain for ever in my mind's eye. It was a presage of greater things to come against the same side. Over 20,000 people watched my first clash with the men from down-under – a third of Northampton's season attendance, and a fifth of the population of the town! Never before that day had I seen so many in the Wantage Road ground, and never since that day have so many passed through the same gates to watch a match. It was one of the few occasions I have ever felt the Northamptonshire ground possessed a real cricketing atmosphere.

My excitement mounted with the crowd's as the sides lined up and were presented to the Duke of Gloucester.

Who knew, perhaps on this day I would bowl out the Australians and fulfil my childish dreams? The weather was bright, and the wicket looked firm and fast, as Freddie Brown won the toss and put Australia in to bat. Arthur Morris was a puzzled man when he returned to the pavilion after losing the toss. He must have thought the Northampton and England captain had taken leave of his senses to have made such a decision. He little knew what was about to happen.

As Freddie Brown handed me the cherry-red new ball, I was miles away, deep in thought. Life is funny, I mused. Only two days ago, I was playing cricket at college and now here I am bowling against the Aussies. It is quite a promotion. I shook my head clear of such thoughts and turned to measure out my seventeen-pace run.

Arthur Morris turned and watched me striding out, away from where he stood at the bowling wicket. I could almost read his thoughts:

'Here's another joker who runs faster than he can bowl.' He is in for a rude awakening, I thought.

The slips were ready, Colin McDonald had taken up his stance, and the crowd settled back to watch the so-called new fast bowler Northampton had acquired.

It was Newbolt who wrote of the 'breathless hush in the close'. Reading of it is but a pale substitute for the experience. The silence is tangible, full of excitement and charged with expectancy. As I ran up to bowl, the crowd's electric murmur died to nothing and even as my arm came over and the match started, they were wondering if I could possibly be as fast as I looked.

I was. The first ball was a fast full-toss, which took McDonald's sluggish bat high on the edge of the blade.

It hit the pickets at deep third-man before anyone could move a muscle. I had been hit for four first ball! It was an indignity not to be suffered. I was muttering to myself in anger as I stomped back to my bowling mark, and the slip-fielders began to edge respectfully away. Already I was unwisely trying to bowl as fast as I could. I would teach him to hit me for four! Four short steps, and feet splayed, I reached long and stretched into my approach. My body rose and tensed as I neared the stumps, and I rocked back as if trying to touch the ground behind me. The ball was straight, and as fast as I could make it. It was on a length and McDonald playing back was visibly late on his stroke. The painful thud of ball on pad blended with my rapturous appeal and the umpire's finger shot up without hesitation. Honour had been satisfied, and McDonald limped off, a lone figure against the background roar of the crowd, who had only just realised what had happened. The ball lay where it had fallen, red and accusing, dead in line with the middle stick. As my team-mates gathered round in congratulation, I realised that history and the Indian match of the previous year was repeating itself. I only hoped that I could press home my initial advantage.

Meanwhile the next man in a green cap had come out of the pavilion, walked to the wicket and taken guard. Quiet once more descended on the crowd, as I prepared to bowl the last balls of the over, Graeme Hole, a beautiful player to watch when in full cry, was at the wicket. He was a stylist, whose bat's swing was long and straight, and whose backlift, his Achilles heel, was invitingly high. If only I could pitch a fast yorker, I yearned.

Gripping the seam with my fore- and index-finger, I prepared to blast Graeme from his block hole. My leg came down stiff and jarring on the popping-crease and my thunderbolt had been fired. It was the last ball of the over, and the South Australian played late and hard at a line outside the off-stump. The ball pitched short of a length; he snicked it with the inside edge of the bat and his middle stump crunched sickeningly to the ground!

For a moment I was aware of nothing but pandemonium. It was incredible but true. I had taken two wickets in my first over against the Aussies! Keith Andrew wandered over, bemused, and shook me by the hand. I do not think he could believe it any more than I could. To this day he has never forgotten his first match with Northamptonshire, and always refers to it as one of his unforgettable moments in cricket.

My success was brief but startling. It could not last and it did not, and Australia's revenge followed swiftly in the wake of my opening shocks. Enter Neil Harvey to collect a complete, compact, century. Arthur Morris, who had been a spectator of the opening fireworks, contributed a battered and bruised 80. Each time I struck him, he looked at Freddie Brown meaningly, as if to say: 'you so and so, now I know why you put us in to bat'. Freddie Brown grinned back and, on occasions, even went over to Arthur solicitously. But even as he helped to rub the afflicted member he was laughing and his smile seemed to say: 'Well Arthur, we have been taking this since the war. How do you like your own medicine?'

Northamptonshire lost the match by an innings, but I was happy. My one bowl had only yielded two wickets for 62, – but in my heart of hearts, I knew I could bowl out more of the Australians. That night I went to sleep, saying to myself: 'Just you wait, Australia, just you wait!'

I think I never realised just how fast I was in those days, but it was not long before I began to make other people realise it. A most unpleasant lifting wicket gave Lancashire every reason to regret that they had let me go to Northamptonshire. There was never any danger of my bowling the Lancashire batsmen out, but it was the closest I have ever come to killing a batsman. Ball after ball lifted from a length to whistle over the batsmen's heads. Very early in the innings I broke Geoffrey Edrich's hand, but he carried on the tradition of his family's guts by batting on.

This, I thought, was open defiance, and I really let the next one go, pitching it just short of a length. Geoff did not even have to duck. The ball steepled from a length and Brian Reynolds, behind the sticks, rose to it like a trout taking a fly. But the ball refused to be caught and, passing over the tips of his outstretched fingers, it bounced once and hit the boundary boards. I had nearly bowled six byes!

My speed has always come from my shoulders, and in my early days I had a tendency to be a slinger pure and simple. My arm was low and did not pass close to my head; my action was more like the sideways sling of a discus-thrower than a fast bowler, and my back leg often swung in a scythe-like movement, kicking down the bowler's wicket.

These characteristics combined to make me erratic, for it is proportionally and generally true that the lower the bowler's arm, the less accurate the ball. I remember reading that in the early days of round-arm bowlers there were invariably a large number of wides on the score-card. The reason is obvious; with a low arm sling, there is only one split second to release the ball. Hang on too long and the ball will be wide on the off. Let go too early and the trajectory of the arm takes the ball wide on the leg.

Most fast bowlers are taught to bowl across the front foot and point that foot towards leg-slip. Most fast bowlers, that is, except me. My front foot always pointed, and still does when I bowl, towards the off-side: my left side was never braced, and I had a tendency to be open-chested at the moment of delivery. This pecularity has defied the efforts of all coaches from Gover downwards, and I am rather attached to my idiosyncrasy. In my early days, to have tampered with my action might have lessened my speed, since it created a tremendous whip-like tension in my right side which, like the action of a javelin thrower, catapulted the ball at the batsman.

This speed has always been my saving grace. If there is one quality for which the cricket watchers of the world will remember me, it will not be for my swing nor my less-than-classical action, it will be because I was fast; and when I was fresher to cricket, I was faster.

I can recall Emrys Davies opening for Glamorgan in one of my first games in county cricket. He was fifty and I was a mere twenty-three. At the end of his knock, some few minutes and no runs later, he walked to the pavilion and announced he was going to retire from county cricket. I had bowled him with a fast full-toss, and he openly confessed he had not seen the ball.

'When that happens,' added Em, 'it's time to retire!'

It may well be I shall be remembered as one of the fastest bowlers ever to appear for England. I shall certainly be on Northamptonshire's records as one of their fastest. Over a period of four years I served England well. How I wish I could say the same about my county of adoption, for I have never been a good servant of Northamptonshire. My bowling average for England is far better than that for my county. I wonder if the Northampton spectators over the years have ever been puzzled by my seeming inability to take five wickets whilst they were watching. I do not think I have performed the feat more than half a dozen times in seven years before the home crowd.

The truth is that the Northampton wicket has never given me the chance to distinguish myself. In all my years with the county, only just over a dozen fast bowlers have captured the elusive five at Northampton. This is not just a loud lament: it is a fact.

When I first came to the midland county, the pitches had so little pace and were so good that quite often visiting sides had to be content with one innings matches, and a titanic struggle for first innings points. In one season alone, we had thirteen draws, most of them at home. It was hardly the type of cricket that drew the crowds and filled the grounds. Desperate situations demanded desperate counter-measures, and the Northamptonshire policy-makers, deluded by the idea that results meant brighter cricket, began to cater for their strong suit, spin-bowlers. The groundsman was ordered to prepare spinning wickets by scraping off the grass and leaving the wicket bare on a spin-bowler's length. It was rather amusing to look at a Northampton wicket of the '56, '57 era; it had the piebald appearance of a pitch with grass everywhere except on the slow-bowlers' length. It was a policy that yielded results, and if one took the attitude that the end justified the means, then Northamptonshire were a good side.

For me it was a frustrating period. Here was I, an England bowler, currently in the international sides, touring

South Africa and Australia with the M.C.C., being used as a bowler whose primary use was to remove the shine from the new ball so that the spinners could grip it to bowl. It was a situation that had its advantages, for I was seldom tired after bowling at Northampton. For two years the home matches followed a monotonous routine: after an 11.30 start, I would be handed the new ball and allowed to bowl two overs to remove the polish. We never bothered to play a second fast bowler since it was deemed a waste of a bowler and a chance to strengthen the batting by the inclusion of another batsman. Quite often the opening partner of the current England quick bowler was a spinner or a batsman who bowled a few medium-pace balls to make way for George Tribe at 11.45. I honestly doubt whether, in those days, Northamptonshire needed even one quick bowler. I am absolutely certain that they did not deserve one.

Under such conditions, if I were England's current quick bowler, I could not expect to remain so for long. After all a bowler has to practice. In many ways, I had only myself to blame for the situation. I had been warned. Len Hutton, after his retirement from Test cricket following the Australian tour, played for Yorkshire in several games. One of them was at Northampton, played on a 'cabbage patch special'. At this time it was the current joke amongst the Northamptonshire boys that cabbages could be planted in the wicket without any further preparation. After the match, Len took me on one side.

'If you carry on playing for this side,' he said, 'You will be out of Test cricket in two years. Go back to Lancashire.'

How I wish I had taken his advice. He was so right.

Often I wonder whether things would have taken another course if I had not renewed my contract following my victorious tour of Australia. Would it have been worth feeling guilty at the thought that after all Northamptonshire did give me a chance where Lancashire had refused? And could I have been sure that Northamptonshire would have let me go to my native county? It is an alarming thought that, though the move would have been in the interests of English cricket, yet in all probability permission would have been denied, and Northampton would have placed its own interests before those of England and her fast bowler. Is it possible to foster and build up the best English team under such conditions? I doubt it.

All this is pure hypothesis – the big 'if'. What is more certain is that counties which, like Northamptonshire, prepared, prepare, and are willing to prepare, wickets to the exclusive liking of their own bowlers, are doing English cricket a grave disservice. It is not surprising that touring sides that come to our shores are baffled by our slow turning wickets. In my experience, we are the only country in the world where these unfair pitches are made by design, and with malice aforethought. It is impossible to play sporting cricket on them since they favour the spin-bowler without giving the batsman a chance to hit back. Even when the ball is right up to the bat, and there is apparently no danger in the innocent delivery, the striker hesitates to go for the logical shot, because he knows that the slowness of the ball off the pitch makes it impossible to stroke it away. The only hope of scoring lies in a full-blooded crack at a delivery which may stop on him or turn enough to find the edge, which will sky it high in the air. Because such pitches encourage the spin-bowler, they breed a race of crease-bound English batsmen, who are completely at sea when they come to bat on firm, unyielding, and bouncy overseas wickets. Who can blame the English player, when he knows full well that if he leaves his crease and fails by inches to get to the pitch of the ball, he is out? What a spectacle we often make of ourselves in Australia, where the leg-spinner, though he does not deviate very much, makes the ball bounce enough to clip the top of English bats and carry to first-slip.

Much has been said and even more written about brighter cricket. What a pity nothing constructive has ever been attempted! No one in this country, apparently, has ever seriously tried to put into practice what they have so often advocated: the preparation of fast wickets. What the game wants more than anything else is a pitch that gives an equal chance to bat and ball: a wicket where the batsman has no need to pound the ball away, but can stroke it to the pickets. A quick wicket will give the fast bowler a chance while the effect of the roller lies still heavy upon it, and when the second and third days come along, a bone hard surface often crumbles to help the spinner.

This has been apparent for many years to everyone – to everyone, that is, except the M.C.C.'s brighter cricket council. I suppose in the course of twenty years there have been almost a dozen changes in the rules to foster brighter cricket. In the late 'twenties the leg-before-wicket ruling was altered, and since that time legislation for brighter cricket has snowballed. Now there is a smaller ball in use, leg-side fielders are limited, and the number behind the stumps on that side of the wicket are limited to two. I often wondered as a boy, which came first: the chicken or the egg? Now I find myself wondering whether the actual game of cricket was thought of before the rules. Picture the poor umpire treading his troubled way to the middle of the cricket field. What, do you think, is he wondering and puzzling over? In his pocket he carries a piece of heavy metal designed specially to tell the 'dragger' where he must start his drag. He informs the bowler that in no circumstances must his trailing foot cut the bowling-crease, and if his front foot crosses the popping-crease, he will be warned, then no-balled. The rest of his duties are less onerous, for apart from the common decisions he has to make, he has now only to decide whether the bowler is running on the wicket and, if he is bowling intimidatory bouncers at the poor, oppressed batsman. During his spare moments at square-leg he has nothing to do except to make sure that the bowler at the other end is not throwing; a perfectly simple undertaking. The joys of umpiring are not for me. I should be afraid I should have to employ the services of a geometrician and legal adviser. More than that, I cannot help wondering if the ordinary spectator would not be happier if we allowed bowlers to pitch the odd fast delivery from eighteen yards.

Does anyone think it is possible to legislate for brighter cricket? To my mind it would be comparable with saying: 'And the M.C.C. said "let cricket be bright", and it was bright.' If it is possible to make rules for brighter cricket, why is it that now, after twenty years of experiment and its resulting labyrinth of laws, the chap who pays his two bob at the gate is still the most neglected person on county cricket grounds? He pops into the grounds, not so much expecting, as hoping rather pathetically, to be entertained. The first-class cricketer does not regard himself as an entertainer, nor does he pay very much attention to the little man on the pickets. Why should he? The person who pays the pro's wages is not the little man on the boundaries, it is the big man on the committee; the selector who picks him for the county and, should he be good enough, the England teams. Oh what a blunder this is! We, in cricket, are years behind our times, still playing the game for the pleasure of the few privileged ones who can afford to take days off to watch mid-week games. What would happen to the Variety star who only tried to please the man who gave him his money, and ignored the public at large. I rather fancy his popularity would be short-lived!

To survive, I feel that cricket has to choose between cutting down expenses and becoming a more popular game and entertainment. There is no doubt that we are living in the age of high wage bills, large professional staffs, and costly maintenance of grounds. The overheads involved in running a county cricket team are enormous, and just to open the gates of the Melbourne Cricket Ground, in preparation for an M.C.C. match, costs over £500.

How are we going to meet such high overheads? In the old days there was the rich patron who could make good the club's deficit, and reassure the bank that an overdraft would be met. Nowadays, of course, rich patrons and spare thousands of pounds are hard to come by, and though the subsidy of the football pool has stepped into many a breach, I am far from reassured about the economic future of the game. Not all the county clubs have football pools, and without them it is likely that many will go to the wall, and the seventeen members of the Championship will be considerably reduced in number.

The problem is how to make county cricket pay its way. The simple method would be to draw more people through the turnstiles by making the games more interesting. Baseball in America is so popular because it provides entertainment over a set period of time and gives a definite result. By comparison with such stuff, a three-day cricket match is a tedious battle of attrition, unenjoyable to player and spectator alike. The irony of the system is that two-thirds of the game is often wasted in a meaningless titanic struggle for first innings points, and only on the third day do the sides finally get down to the business of reaching a definite result. I shall never know why the whole system is not revised, and the public offered a one-day game, a one-innings game, on the one day they can watch it. If the match were played at the week-end, it would be certain of the biggest possible crowds, and with semi-professional and part-time players the costs would be reduced to a sensible level. With present-day economic trends in county cricket I feel certain that the hour of week-end cricket is at hand.

Even if we deal with the financial problems facing cricket, the question-mark against brighter cricket still remains. If players become less dependent upon the game for a livelihood, I am certain it will have the salutary effect of making them think that after all cricket is only a game and one to be enjoyed by player and public alike. It is this attitude which is necessary in present-day cricket if we are going to make even the professional game more palatable to the general public. It has been the source of constant amazement to me that the Lords of Lord's have never circularised the players, to inform them that after all cricket is more than a tradition, it is an entertainment which, alas, today has to pay its way. I cannot bring myself to believe that the people in charge of English cricket are bad businessmen, yet such is the inference, for they have made no effort to attract the crowds. True, the game has been only a hobby-horse to most of our administrators, and one which they rode, in many instances, twenty years ago. The game itself has altered little in that time, but can it be possible that there exist people who do not realise that public taste has changed considerably? It is an unfortunate present-day truth, that a concern that costs money and requires ability to run must have able men at the top and make a profit. How much administrative cricket ability is there in England? I should hesitate to pass judgment, and must content myself with telling the story of the committeeman who, when I was bowling at my fastest, approached me and asked if I was turning my quicker ball very much!

If the administrators of English cricket are not aware of their obligations to the general public, how are we going to make the professional county cricketer realise it is his duty to amuse the crowd? His whole existence is bounded by figures and results, and not by the way he plays cricket. The pro has one eye on his salary and one on his thousand runs and hundred wickets. In present-day England it is a disaster to lose a Test Match. I am reminded of the American businessman who, during a visit to England, got off the boat-train at Waterloo, to be faced with enormous placards which announced: 'Total collapse of England. England faces disaster.'

'Had the national economy received its death blow?' he asked.

No, England were just batting badly in the Test Match.

He had discovered that many Englishmen, like the Yorkshireman, do not play cricket just for fun.

Yet it is possible to bridge that gap between playing to win and playing to entertain. When Denis Compton took his side to South Africa in 1959 he instructed us to go into the middle and try to amuse the crowd. Only three years previously, Tayfield's bowling had tied him to the crease, but now he danced down the wicket and dispatched him to all quarters of Kent Park. At one stage of the match, with their side struggling to escape defeat by an innings, Tom Graveney and Brian Close added 125 in the hour before lunch. The crowds poured in to watch the fun, and it was small wonder, when two teams who were determined to have a good game got together and served champagne-cricket.

How often do we see such cricket in England? I hazard to answer not very often, though I like to think that in spite of the slow wicket at Northampton, we have produced more than our share of the brighter type of cricket. This being the case, I have often been puzzled why Northamptonshire, who over the years have had a strong side, have not been consistently higher in the Championship table. It is a question which is often asked of me, and not without reason, for to all competent judges, Northamptonshire is a far better side than its performances suggest. Over the past few years we have consistently beaten the then current Champion county, Surrey, more times than they have beaten us, and Northamptonshire has not been without its successes against the stronger counties of Lancashire, Yorkshire, and Middlesex. Why then have we not done better?

Certainly it cannot be that the county has not had the

individual players capable of championship performances. Denis Brookes, or Brookey to his friends, has been one of the best opening bats in the country for years, and his sergeant-major stance and knowledge of the game were looked up to wherever cricket was played. Perhaps we did not have our Mr Stanley, but we certainly possessed our Dr Livingstone, and Jock's ability to play spin-bowling was second to none in the world. Maybe he did hit across the line of the ball slightly, but it is an undeniable fact, and his records prove it, that he almost invariably made contact. When Northampton people speak of all-rounders, they speak of the complete all-rounder, George Tribe, in the same breath, for to them he personified the whole span of Northamptonshire criket for eight years. Raman Subba Row, the present Northants skipper, has been on two M.C.C. tours and so has Keith Andrew. It may be true that Raman is an ungainly player who scores most of his runs by deflections and nudges, but his application, concentration and determination are such that he is one of the most difficult players in the country to dislodge. When Jack Manning transferred his allegiance to Northamptonshire from his native South Australia, he probably threw away a golden chance to play for Australia both at home and abroad. Certainly I have never met a left-arm spinner who has given the ball a bigger 'tweak' than Jack. The county's senior professional, Des Barrick, was on the very verge of the England side which went to the West Indies in 1953, and Micky Allen has played in more than one game for M.C.C. at home.

With this wealth of cricketing talent it is incredible that Championship honours should have eluded the midland county for so long. Where shall we look for the reason for this apparent failure? Individual ability is not enough, for the success of any team lies beyond the single unit: it lies in the composite effect of many units welded together into a whole. Success comes to the team, and not to a collection of gifted and talented individuals, however good they may be. In every game of cricket, in my experience, it has always been the better team that won, and it is this unity that in my opinion has been missing from Northamptonshire cricket.

A cricketer who has the distinction of playing for Yorkshire or Lancashire is a prophet in his own land and is looked up to and respected as a representative of his county. In return, he himself is proud to wear the Red or White Rose on his cap, and under such conditions it is not difficult to induce a spark of team spirit into the units of the side. Imagine how hard it is to coax team spirit into a side where county pride and respect are non-existent, and where representing one's county has as much significance as catching the 8.30 train to the office. In his recent book Jim Laker reports the incident of the Northants player who, when he should have been playing against Surrey, was busy in his garden. Jim misses the very salient point that the selectors, who had not picked the player for the previous match, had not informed him of his subsequent selection, but very astutely notices that the man himself was not moved by any motives of loyalty to inquire whether he has been chosen for the county side or not. At least he could have turned up at the ground to find out if he was playing. Though it would be wrong to take this case as typical, it does indicate what pride the individual player takes in the fact that he plays for Northamptonshire. The people who represent the county on the cricket field, almost without exception, hail from places outside Northamptonshire. To say the least they are a mixed bunch, and include in their number New Zealanders, Australians, West Indians, South Africans, Lancastrians, Yorkshiremen, Northumbrians, men from Surrey, Shropshire, Bedford, Norfolk, and Uncle Tom Cobley and all. At one stage there was a wild rumour in the dressing-room that our next recruit would be an Eskimo! Keith Andrew and I founded a club called, appropriately enough, the Cosmo Club to foster team spirit in our polyglot side, and to get the boys together off the field for a talk and a drink, so that gradually cricket on the middle would become more a question of playing together. But to turn a cosmopolitan team such as ours into a fighting unit is a task that equals one of the labours of Hercules. As long as the minority of the side are natives of Northamptonshire; as long as the only attraction for talent that comes from outside the county is money; as long as the county committee will pay that money; and as long as there remains a difference in the basic wages of first-team professional players just so long will there be petty jealousies between player and player, and an absence of team spirit. It seems so silly when one realises that the individual's interests are best served by the success of the team as a whole. The cricketer who is a member of the Championship-winning combination is invariably at the top of his own professional tree.

I hope that the best possible construction will be placed upon my criticisms, for my aim is to assist the side that, after all, gave me my first chance in county cricket. In the very near future, Northamptonshire will face, together with many other of the weaker counties, one of the biggest crises of its modern revival. The days of farming surplus playing strength from the larger counties are over, and teams such as Yorkshire and Lancashire will guard their players closely lest they lose more Lakers and Tysons. More and more counties like my own must come to foster their own boys and build up the fighting qualities of a true Northamptonshire side. The future of such counties no longer lies in the broad acres of Yorkshire or among the mill chimneys of Lancashire; it has come to rest heavily and squarely on the shoulders of their coaching staffs. The future teams of Northamptonshire will be just as good as their coaches.

I wish them well, for it was they who first gave me a crack at international cricket. Had it not been for them, and Bill Edrich's broken cheek-bone, the Test Match world might never have seen the rise of the Tyson star. It is strange to think that it was not any great bowling performance that claimed my place on the Australian boat in 1954, but purely the fact that I had broken Bill Edrich's cheek-bone in the Northamptonshire match against Middlesex. If there is a true adage in the English cricket world, it is that if you want to get on in the game, the place to bowl well is at Lord's, before the eyes of the mighty. How well I remember that sunny July day in 1954, when, if I did not bowl well, I certainly bowled very fast! The match seemed as if it was going to be a blood bath when Middlesex batted, for in the first over there was already a pool of blood on the wicket – not of any victim of mine, but from the split chin of our wicket-keeper, Keith Andrew. Edrich came to the wicket after I had quickly disposed of Jack Robertson and Harry Sharp. He was still in his prime as a hooker and player of fast bowling. Bill the hooker, I thought, I'll give him hook! In my first over to him, I gave

Bill a bouncer and, fearless as ever, he made an ill-advised attempt to hook it. He was fractionally late on the shot and the ball took him full on the cheek with a crunching sound. He fell like a pole-axed ox, to be carried off the field unconscious and spend an uncomfortable night in hospital. Once more there was blood on the wicket.

Denis Compton, though he was next in to bat, was in the shower at the time, and came to the dressing-room window.

'Cor,' he said, 'just think how fast he will be at Sydney! Sorry, Peter', he added, turning to Peter DeLisle, the young Oxford batsman, 'I'm not ready. You'll have to go in!' Peter made his way trembling to the blood and sawdust-covered wicket.

One month later I was playing in my first Test Match against Pakistan at The Oval. My boat ticket to Australia was already in my pocket. I had come a long way in twelve months.

CHAPTER TEN

# The Feeling Changes

When I first set pen to paper in my unusual course of writing my own cricket memoirs, I little dreamt that my greatest literary problem would spring from the fact that success in the cricket world came to me too early in my career. In the material world of financial reward, there can be no such thing as success which comes too early, but in the sphere of human drama and biography, achievement born too early is but the premature crisis of the plot, and instead of climax is an anticlimax. Thereafter everything is but the gradual winding-down and decline of interest raised too quickly and killed too suddenly. Would Shakespeare's *Romeo and Juliet* have been a masterpiece of human tragedy if the curtain of the second act had revealed the star-crossed lovers already lying dead on the stage? The question is purely rhetorical.

Success in my first tour of Australia was the climax of my career and already the *dénouement* of my plot was upon me and the play almost over before it had begun. Now began the struggle to make the climax continue for the rest of the play, and I very quickly found out that the problem of getting to the top in cricket is child's play compared to the task of remaining there.

The Press criticisms were favourable, and a long run seemed assured; but one should learn not to put one's trust in the princes of Fleet Street. It had only seemed like yesterday that the headlines which now read 'Tyson the magnificent' had told a different story. 'Send Tyson home', had been the opinion of one tabloid which now proclaimed its past faith in my ability as a great fast bowler. I have often wished I had the conscience of a newspaper cricket writer. What a life it must be to follow the sun in search of sport, and what an easy conscience one must have, to share the drinking hour before dinner with a player you have attacked in tomorrow's paper! It is undoubtedly true that what the public reads today, it nearly always forgets tomorrow – all the public, that is, except one person.

An amoral outlook is not easy to forgive, but it is easy to understand. After all, the majority of cricket writers merely toe the party line and follow policy laid down by the editors. The attitude of any sports writer to a question is necessarily dictated by the paper he writes for, and the interests concerned are not those of the welfare of cricket but the problem of selling papers and giving the public what the public wants to read.

I remember how in 1958, when the second Test had reached a particularly interesting stage and Australia was just about to take the initiative, Peter Richardson appeared at breakfast dressed for a hot day, in a red shirt and without either tie or coat. Many of the Australian hotels insist upon strict propriety in the matter of dress and refuse to serve meals to people who do not wear ties and coats, and Peter was accordingly told to return to his room and put on these items of clothing. It hardly seems possible that such a trivial incident should take precedence over the more serious business of a Test Match, yet such was the case. The fact that Peter Richardson had been told to return to his room and make the required change of clothes made headlines in the evening paper. It was news.

There are too many reporters who put the news value of cricket before objective reporting of any game. In a way the cricketers themselves are to blame, for it is very rarely that the scribes have any opportunity to enthuse over the game itself, but the hypercritical and newshound attitude towards cricket carries the seeds of it own destruction. One cannot keep on hitting out at the game while it is on the floor without eventually impairing or destroying it, and it seems the height of folly to me that anyone, newspaperman or not, should want to put an end to the game that, indirectly, gives him his own living.

At least one can take consolation in the fact that theirs is an outlook which sells newspapers, even though it does not help cricket. It indicates that in their own sphere they are better businessmen than the administrators of cricket.

In my years of success the minions of Fleet Street were, not unnaturallly, in my favour, and thoughts of the insecurity of my position never crossed my mind. How could my position as England's leading fast bowler be in jeopardy when the laurels of success had only just been placed on my brow and when, after all, there were only five fast bowlers to challenge my place in the touring Test team? The thought was laughable. So was my complacency.

I little realised the hazards which lie in the paths of cricketers who hope for consistent choice in the England home team. As yet I was new to the arena of Test cricket and had not awoken to the fierceness of competition between the two hundred, and not twenty, English cricketers, who struggle for places in the elusive eleven. The player who represents England abroad has an easy conscience compared with the man who is selected at home. For the tourist, the main element of chance lies in his original choice for the touring team. Thereafter the sides are selected by the senior players – people in a position to assess your cricketing capabilities, since they are on the field of play with you. At home, Test teams are chosen by the vagaries of the selectors, who are completely unable to cover the full scope of English cricket since it is too comprehensive, and are inevitably pulled by strings of loyalty to favour players who hail from their own counties. It is favouritism which is entirely natural, and understanderably subconscious. I know full well that I stood a far better chance of being picked for England as long as Northamptonshire had a voice in the selection committee in the person of Freddie Brown. He had seen me at my best and my worst, but he had at least *seen* me regularly.

The only touchstone for England selection at home is that of current form. In most cases ability will out, and performances in county cricket consistently and correctly indicate the better players. Yet frequently current form can be a myth, since it is so often qualified by local conditions. There is, for example, a considerable difference between bowling at Trent Bridge or Northampton and bowling at Lord's. The Trent Bridge wicket and the Northampton pitch are notoriously devoid of the life and pace that helps all fast bowlers. When one bowls at Lord's, though there is not always pace in the wicket, there is always the slope towards the Tavern which moves the ball down the hill, off the seam. Looking back objectively over the years immediately following my successful tour of Australia, I can now realise, without rancour, that when Len Hutton told me I should be out of the England side within two years if I continued at Northampton, he was not making a forecast. He was stating a logical fact. The basic truth was, that it was impossible for me to challenge for a place in the England side at home on the strength of current form. Northamptonshire play nine of their home fixtures on the town ground, and since the trend at home was to prepare turning wickets – on which I bowled, on an average, six overs per match – it was almost impossible, in the seasons of the Northamptonshire deserts, for me to bowl sufficient overs either to claim a hundred wickets, or seriously challenge for a Test place. Any pretensions I might have had were entirely dependent upon my performances away from home, and were confined to seventeen matches.

Excuses such as these slip easily from the tongue, and salve my own feelings, but while they are undoubtedly true, they do not account in full for my fall from grace. I must acknowledge that I was not equal to the stiff task of staying at the top in England. The brutal truth about my bowling at home was that it was not good enough. If I have heard people ask once whether I was losing my speed, I must have heard the question a thousand times. It is so easy to forget that good fast bowling in this country does not depend on speed alone. If that had been the case, I should have been supreme in England for many years, and faster than most bowlers when I retired. Even now I know that I can still bowl very fast when I want to. No, Frank Tyson never lost his ability to hurl them down as fast as he ever used to, he just awoke to the fact that on English wickets speed is not the complete answer to the problem of getting the ball past the bat. Imagine the bowler who stalks back to the end of his twenty-yard run, turns and moves into his approach, smooth, low and accelerating, until he springs in a final fine frenzy of energy to fling the ball down at the batsman; it pitches just short of a length with a plop, loses half its pace and refuses to bounce more than half-stump high! The immediate reaction of the bowler is to ask himself what is the point of trying to bowl fast. In Australia, when I pitched the ball short it bounced, and the angle of its accidence was almost equal to that of its incidence, but in England a bouncer was quite often a waste of energy.

Something more than pure speed was necessary to beat the bat, and it was far better to cut down pace if this would enable me to swing or move the ball more off the pitch. The great fast bowlers in this country have always been those who had the little extra quality. In Lindwall it was his native boomerang swing and his guile; Larwood had pin-point accuracy and a late movement in the air. At the other end of the scale, the bowlers who were not even fast, yet moved the ball, always enjoyed greater success in England than those who relied purely on the penetrative quality of pace. One could cite the Hampshire stalwart, Len Shackleton, as a case in point.

Many spectators think that it is Brian Statham's pace alone that brings him his annual crop of a hundred wickets. If pace were the only weapon in his armoury, I can assure you that his plentiful years would have been seasons of famine. Speaking as an unworthy batsman, yet one whom the laws of cricket compel to bat, I can assure you that the Greyhound's successes spring from the batsmen's knowledge that almost every ball will pitch on the stumps; that Brian can throw in a yorker whenever he wants; and that often the striker is left stranded in mid-stroke when a ball he was trying to force on the off-side has suddenly whipped treacherously back off the seam to bowl him.

Yorkshire's Fred Trueman may be ferocious in attitude, but I hazard a guess that a few years have passed since Fred was at his fast and fiery best. Though he has always been fairly fast, the most powerful shot in his locker has always been his natural inborn ability to swing the ball away from the bat and in recent years he has only paid lip-service to his emphasis on speed. On good wickets the yeasty Yorkshireman is content to bowl five overs off his long run, before reducing his approach and his speed to concentrate on bowling swingers. He has chosen well, for there is not a better swinger of the ball in the world.

Mine has never been the ability to swing the ball like Trueman, nor seam it like Statham, and so, in the years following my meteoric rise, it was frustrating for me to know that, although I was not a worse or slower bowler, my weapon of speed was less effective in England than in Australia. The unfounded whisper was that I was losing my pace. In one respect it was true. I had decided consciously to cut down my pace in an effort to do more with the ball. To swing the ball at Northampton was almost out of the question; the dusty nature of the wicket meant it was only possible to keep the shine on the ball for four overs. Since the wicket was helpful to spinners, I began to experiment with leg-cutters; a delivery which, while not a true spinner, is yet spun slightly by a cutting, rolling movement of wrist and fingers over the seam of the ball, and turns slightly from leg at medium-pace. Little did I realise it, but the learned committeeman's inquiry was becoming a prophecy. I was trying to turn my fast one!

Maturity brings cunning to the fast bowler, and adds yet another facet to his nature, other modes of attack to his repertoire. Yet the coming of guile to quick bowling can be like the advance of creeping paralysis to the body. Outwardly, thought and cunning methods add to the armoury of the quick bowler, and make him the complete, shrewd, mechanically perfect athlete. Inwardly, guile saps the psychological foundations of the edifice of fast bowling until it takes away the real desire and the very reasons for wanting to bowl quick. When I began to bowl on the Northampton pitch, it did not matter that the wicket was slow, for I was young and full of unquenchable optimism and enthusiasm. Five years of bowling later, I was a changed man. At first it was just a thought, small at first, but ever nibbling at my consciousness – why should I bowl fast on that so-and-so wicket? If I dig a really quick one in, it only comes off half stump high at medium pace. Bowling fast on that is a waste of time. I will cut down my speed and try to swing the ball more in the air. Perhaps I could move the ball more off the seam if I were slower, and when the pitch is favourable to spinners, I could try a few leg-cutters. Oh, I fooled myself that should the fast wicket come along, and should there be any need to bowl fast again, I could turn on the pace just like turning on a tap. But without enthusiasm it is not easy to bowl fast. I told myself I could never lose the ability to throw the odd thunderbolt down: that fast bowlers are born and not made. For the moment, though, I seemed to be wasting my time and energy on pitches made of cotton wool. Slowly, ever so slowly, the desire, incentive and will to bowl fast evaporated and with it went the real and precious gift of being able to do so. The dyed-in-the-wool character faded, and with him vanished his enthusiasm and ability. Real fast bowling was hard work, and what was once a pleasure was now a job.

While enthusiasm still lingered, so did genuine ability, and even in England there were times when I touched the Olympian heights of my Australian tour, and thought that the touch of inspiration had not yet fled. I can still remember the games when the old rhythm seemed to return; the times when my left leg braced itself and stiffened preparatory to lifting my body to its pinnacle of power, whence it smashed down the ball at the cowering batsman. Genuine pace died only slowly, in proportion to my diminishing stomach for the sweaty hard work of bowling fast.

One such occasion was the South African Test Match at Nottingham in 1955. I suppose the match could really be classified in my Australian period, as I had only been home for about three months. Another qualifying circumstance was the fact that I bowled on a rain-affected wicket, which helped me considerably. But in spite of these things, it was one of the few occasions when my England form has borne any relation to my bowling in Australia in 1954. I really felt good, effective, rhythmic, fast and unjaded.

John Arlott had always worked on the theory that I performed better on the cricket field after a night of drinking red wine, and on the Sunday previous to my bowling on the Monday, he had more than played his part in strengthening England's hand. The following day even the ball felt good in my hand. Right from the word go, my stride was smooth, long and cadenced, and there was a feeling of purpose and speed in my bowling. Over the week-end, South Africa were 46 for no wicket. Though this situation was not destined to last, it was not until the run-ups had dried out and I was in my second spell of bowling that I was able to do any damage to the edifice of the Springbok's batting. Goddard was run out from the fortuitous boot of the bowler, Wardle, while he was backing up, and I flung myself into the breach this slice of luck had made in the ranks of the enemies' batting.

Johnny Waite was my first victim, when, running purposefully to the wicket and striving to reach for the sky in my delivery stride, I unleashed a ball that, pitching short of a length, reared, catching Waite's glove and dropping gently into Denis Compton's hands at short-leg. It was my first taste of blood, and whetted my appetite. Trevor Bailey accounted for McGlew and Endean, and the procession back to the pavilion had started. Now was the time, I thought, the psychological moment for an all-out attack which would put the enemy back on his heels. For the next forty minutes I bowled as fast as I have ever bowled, and at the end of that time South Africa were all out.

Roy McLean was unlucky. He got a ball which kept low, and his hurriedly stabbed bat could do little but change its course into the hands of Tom Graveney at first-slip. The Springbok captain, Jack Cheetham, was the victim of a break-back which would have done justice to Brian Statham and of which I myself was particularly proud. Even as I was approaching the wicket I was toying with the idea of bowling a slinger. The arm was low, narrowly missing umpire Frank Lee's head, and the ball, pitching six inches outside the off-stump, jumped back, passed between angled bat and pad, flicking an edge in its passage, and flattened the middle-stick! I pirouetted with unsuppressed joy and elation at the success of my stratagem. The next ten minutes were the sort of ecstatic moments which every fast bowler lives for; when he bowls out the opposition as quickly as they come in. Not only did I hit the sticks, but I sent them somersaulting and cart-wheeling back into the ever-open arms of Godfrey Evans. As I walked dizzy and dazed with effort into the pavilion, applauded by the Trent Bridge crowd, I did not know that I had taken six wickets for 28 and returned my best performance since the glorious 5th of January at Melbourne. In the final furious fling, I had taken five for 5 in 7 overs! England were home in yet another Test Match, and it seemed almost impossible to me, as I looked back, that in the nine months since I had first set foot on a Test Match field, I had already taken fifty-two wickets.

I was happy in my success, for I had proved that I could do in England what I had done in Australia. The thoughts which passed through my mind as I sipped an after-the-match beer were pleasant ones. The newspapers in Larwood's home county were already hailing me as another Larwood, and it was the most pleasing praise they could have heaped upon my head. The match had another pleasing aspect. Many of the armchair critics were saying my previous successes had been entirely due to the presence of Brian Statham bowling with great accuracy and little luck at the other end. I am the first to acknowledge my debts to Brian and to admit that my decriers were, in part, correct. But Nottingham proved, to myself if to no one else, that I could turn in the performances entirely on my own ability.

The Nottingham Test, although marking a pinnacle of personal success, had its sad moments. It saw the breakdown and disappearance of Bob Appleyard from the Test Match scene. For me Bob will always epitomise the quality of rectitude: a correctness of action and a pin-point accuracy of length and direction, which had made him a constant threat on baked Australian wickets unresponsive to spin. His arm was a ramrod of rectitude as it swung straight over the top, and his subtle variation of pace often had the batsman groping for the ball long before it arrived. More than any other cricketer I ever met, Bob loved cricket, and in true Yorkshire fashion, he hated to lose. He once made Keith Andrew very angry, when, playing golf, he tried every conceivable gamesmanship gambit to avert defeat. First his clubs were unsatisfactory; then his golfing shoes did not fit, so he took them off and finished the round in stockinged feet. The crowning blow for Keith came when, on the very threshold of defeat, Bob wanted to change the handicaps. His reluctance to be beaten, however, was a very useful characteristic on the cricket field.

I have often kicked myself when my bowling has been wild. It is a frustrating feeling to level one's sights on the middle-stick only to see the ball shoot wide down the leg-side. On those sort of days, it is better to resign oneself to the fact that there is nothing one can do about inaccuracy but to try as hard as possible to correct the fault. On such occasions it is just not your day. Consequently I felt for Bob when, in the Nottingham Test, his bowling was, in most uncharacteristic fashion, all over the place. Full-toss followed long-hop, first on the leg-side and then on the off. Godfrey Evans behind the sticks was bruised black and blue by his efforts to stop the vagaries of Bob's bowling, for though the 'keeper always stood up for the Yorkshire off-spinner, the pace was often well above that normally expected of a slow bowler. Little did Godfrey or I realise that Bob's shoulder muscles had wasted away and that he was destined to spend many months of the next year in hospital.

Injury is far from a pleasant prospect in an English season, particularly for a fast bowler. Even trivial hurts are magnified many times over by the fact that continual six-day-a-week cricket gives no respite to the player, and no time for the injury to recover between games. There is the ever-present temptation to begin playing again before the injury has fully mended. How well I know the sickly feeling of apprehension, when after a forced rest of two or three weeks, the time comes for the try-out of the damaged part. Will the ankle hold up under the strain of bowling? The first ball is a moment of awful anxiety, a sensation that is a cross between the desire to play cricket again and the fear of doing further damage. Slowly at first, nursing the strain, the bowler builds up confidence until the apprehension of the mind disappears with the twinges of physical weakness and he is fully fit once more.

I have had my share of injuries, and like most fast bowlers I have been troubled by my feet. Bowling quick is a most unnatural action and my body has often protested against its ill-usage. The left foot is not designed to be pounded time after time into the hard earth; it is merely to walk on. It was a foot injury which forced 'Lol' Larwood to retire and, like the famous bodyline bowler, I too was hampered by the wear-and-tear on my ankles. By the end of my professional cricket career, I had sprained my ankle six times in bad bowling footholds and each time I bowled, it became swollen to such an extent that eventually I was forced to change my original bowling action to avoid causing it further harm. Though my ankle was to cause more trouble later in the year, my primary concern in the early season of 1955 was an injured heel, a legacy of the hard, jarring Australian wickets. On such pitches boots are quickly hammered out of shape and one loose-fitting boot had caused a bruise on my left foot, deep under the thick callous that guards the heel. The Shoes and Allied Trades Research Association came to my rescue with a specially strong pair of boots, but not before this recurring nuisance had caused me to miss several Test Matches.

Indeed the only other Test Match in which I appeared in the season following my Australian triumphs was the Manchester Test; a game which holds special memories for me since it was the only Test I ever played before my native Lancastrian crowd. The occasion was a bitter-sweet one for me, because, although I bowled reasonably well and long, South Africa squeezed home by three wickets with only minutes to spare. For me it was a game of impressions: of exhaustion and disappointment; of pathos, excitement, and tremendous hitting. I remember my wild anger when Jackie McGlew, who went on to score a hundred, edged a ball from me and was caught behind the wicket only to be given not out by the umpire. There was the slashing, swashbuckling innings of Compton, which yielded 70 in the second innings, and was worth travelling many a mile to see, even if it meant that a Yorkshireman would have to come into Lancashire. Lean, long, and lanky Paul Winslow, the most unprepossessing cricketer in appearance, whose batting was devoid of defence and seemed to have no need of it, struck his way to a Samson century with tremendous blows, the like of which I have never seen. One Herculean heave off Tony Lock soared into the long-on ether and assumed the proportions of a pea before passing over the broadcasting box and bouncing in what must have been the middle of the practice ground, well over 120 yards distant. One of his hits, huge and high, found Alec Bedser, playing in his last Test, circling cumbrously beneath it and failing pathetically by yards to reach it.

During the match Peter Heine was rash enough to bowl me a bouncer, a practice which I had never approved of since Ray Lindwall hit me on the head at Sydney. The ethics of a fast bowler dispatching a bouncer at a fellow-tradesman are a little confused in the world of cricket. Over the course of the years, and since I bowled one at Ray Lindwall, I have learned the painful way that it is not the accepted thing. Only two other 'quickies' have bowled a bumper at me, and one was Peter Heine. All that summer I lay in wait for the fiery Dutchman, and at Scarborough I caught up with him. Although I bowled the lifting ball well wide of the leg-stump, I still could not reach Peter, who almost trod on the corns of the square-leg umpire in his earnest desire to get away. After he had returned, we all laughed and declared the bouncing contest a draw. The other bowler who bounced one at me was another Peter – Peter Loader. I shall never forget his pale appearance when he came to the wicket, bat in hand, to face me, and how his set expression went slowly green when the retaliatory bumper hit his bat handle right in front of his eyes!

In spite of its exciting finish, the Manchester Test left a sour taste in my mouth, for it provided me with two major disappointments. By the time the match ended, almost half the players selected to appear in the subsequent Gentleman and Players match had withdrawn from the game, for various reasons of exhaustion, injury, or convenience. I had always been led to believe it was one of the most important matches of the year, but thereafter I was to regard it in its true light: an unrepresentative, ill-timed and outdated mockery. If the organisation of the game were at fault, however, so was the attitude of some of the players towards it. In a way I could sympathise with them, for it is not good policy to organise a representative game after the tense, tiring business of a Test Match. What I could not understand, however, was the attitude of one England batsman, whose contribution to the English gross score had been 6 runs. His country's Test team had been deservedly defeated in a most exciting game, yet all he could find to say about the whole business was: 'Well I haven't earned my money this game!'

Little did I know it at the time, but I had sprained my ankle once more in the exhausting, exciting climax of the match, and this injury kept me out of cricket for three weeks. I deemed myself fit, however, for the Leeds Test Match and travelled down to Lord's to satisfy the selectors and justify my own confidence by a fitness test. After an exhaustive trial, Gubby Allen asked me whether I could feel my ankle at all. I told the truth and said I could feel it, but only very slightly. His reaction was immediate and decisive, and I was informed that the selectors could not take the risk of playing me. Disappointed though I was, I realised, then as now, that theirs was the right and only decision in the circumstances. But if I were upset, there was another person present who also had a fitness trial and was also disappointed, although for a different reason. Colin Cowdrey had injured his hand batting and as it still pained him considerably, he was anxious not to make himself a liability to the England side by playing at Leeds. In the light of subsequent events, he did not in fact play, but while at Lord's for his fitness trial, Gubby Allen told him that he must play at Leeds at all costs. This point has given me much food for thought. If I accept the principle that injured players, no matter how slight their hurt, must not play in a Test Match, why was the chairman of selectors so anxious Colin should play and I should not? I must be forgiven, if at the time, I had an overwhelming awareness that I was a professional.

My sprained ankle was to cost me dear, for it meant that I fell from the selectors' favour and did not appear in another Test until the final match against the Aussies at the Oval the following year. Even then I must have been very fortunate to be selected, as my current form was far from impressive on Northampton's spinning sands. The psychological effect of bowling on consistently slow and unhelpful pitches was already making itself felt, and I sensed, even at this early date, that somehow I was not the same bowler I had been in Australia. Speed was still there, but it was no longer easy to turn on the pace I wanted, and much of my former aggressive attitude had been channelled into a more scientific approach to fast bowling. I began to be more concerned with the correctness of my action than the paramount aim of getting rid of the so-and-so batsman. I had lost incentive, my rhythm was often lacking, and the tired August feeling frequently came over me in June or July.

Even when Tony Lock conjured a miraculous catch to dismiss McDonald in the Oval Test, I could only think of the dismissal of another hated batsman as a rank full-toss which was lucky to get a wicket. It was as if, like Wordsworth, I wondered:

> '*Whither is fled the visionary gleam?*
> *Where is it now, the glory and the dream?*'

In spite of myself, what had been a wonderful and delightful pastime was gradually becoming everyday hack work.

The final Test of the 1956 Australian series was a strange game. I remember it well because it was the only Test I ever played in with David Sheppard, and I can recall that in my own mind I was strongly opposed to his inclusion. His ability was beyond question, but his form was hypothetical, as he had played less than half a dozen county games that season because of his clerical duties. His inclusion in the side was a guess on the part of the selectors. Like most of their gambles in this, their *annus mirabilis*, it paid dividends, and he scored a meritorious 70 runs. The game was affected by rain, and it was this more than other considerations that brought about a drawn game. The Oval wickets at this time were notorious, turning, and lifting when rain fell on them, and it was therefore an eyebrow-raising sight to see Ian Johnson open the attack with his fast bowlers when England resumed batting after the storm. It was even more of a shock when

Archer began by bowling slow off-cutters, and Davidson launched his offensive, not with his usual fast stuff, but with slow left-arm orthodox leg-spinners. If people ask me whether Ian Johnson spun the ball to any appreciable extent, I refer them to this game when, on a turning wicket and with everything in favour of his off-spinners, he tried every bowler in his side, including his fast men and Jimmy Burke, before he took the ball himself. I am always careful to add in justification, that on hard, true Australian wickets, I rated him among the top flight of slow bowlers by virtue of his variation through the air and his ability to drift the ball imperceptibly towards the omnipresent hands of Australian slip-fielders.

I always find it strange to think that I have not played in another Test Match in England since this game at the Oval. I am forced to admit that, though I have always been well to the fore in the ranks of the English quick bowlers, my current English form has rarely justified a Test place. So my home Test career ended in a paradoxical note of triumph and ludicrousness. The triumph lay in a catch I took off the bowling of Jim Laker to dismiss Ron Archer, that I rate as one of the best I ever gathered. Even on bright sunny days, the Oval is a far from good catching ground and on a dull overcast day such as the last day of the 1956 Test, it can be absolutely impossible. Now I can openly admit that I never saw the catch until it was in my hands. I merely began running as soon as I saw Archer sweep the ball towards where I stood at deep-square-leg. On the radio, Rex Alston was commenting quite calmly:

'Archer has swept that ball off his leg stump down towards the square-leg boundary, where Tyson runs in to field it. He is coming in fast and . . . Good heavens he's caught it!'

Ron Archer departed crestfallen, and Australian hopes of averting defeat sank a little further; the score-board showed that six of their second innings wickets had fallen. As the ground was saturated, liberal carpets of sawdust had been laid everywhere, and the rising wind began to whip wooden particles about the field. Ian Johnson came in, took guard, and immediately protested about the sawdust flying into his eyes. The umpires consulted and, after a long confabulation that completely mystified the crowd, they decided play must continue. I was rather disappointed, as the game was virtually dead and drawn, and it would have been a unique if ludicrous experience to have taken part in a contest whose score-sheet would have read: 'sawdust stopped play.'

I must recognise that it is a sad fact that my bowling never reached the same heights in England as it had done in my first tour of Australia. Though in a diminishing degree, and dimly aware of the fact, I knew that I could still bowl fast, but it was becoming increasingly difficult to turn the faucet which unleashed my pace. More important, it was then that I realised that speed was not everything to the quick bowler who played most of his matches in England, particularly when his home ground was at Northampton. This knowledge was perhaps the worst piece of cricketing education I ever received, for it led me to compromise with slow wickets, and to modify my bowling approach. When guile entered at one door, pace and the will to bowl fast went out of the other. There is no doubt in my mind that the best fast bowler is the man who will not compromise, and who, come hell or high water, will bowl fast all the time, whatever the wicket. But I will add this rider: a fast bowler is a person who thrives on encouragement, and who, if we judge by a famous Yorkshire contemporary 'quickie', often sees the ball lift, swing and seam, even when there is no movement at all. It is too much to expect the real fast bowler to pound out his heart on slow wickets, six days a week, six months a year. Under such conditions we shall still produce quick bowlers, but they will not bowl fast for long. Just as the presence of a train suggests the necessity of tracks, so a fast bowler presupposes the need for fast wickets. Until we produce these pitches, real fast bowlers who continue to be fast, will be as rare in England as the duck-billed platypus.

CHAPTER ELEVEN

# 1958 – Throwing and other Controversies

The 1958 tour to Australia, though not destined to be very successful, was one of the most controversial ever undertaken. At first I was happy to be selected: not only because I deemed myself extremely lucky to be making the trip, but also because I was part of a team I thought to be one of the strongest that has ever left these shores. How wrong I was only time would show. I looked back with confidence on England's record over the years 1953 to 1958. In that short space of time the home country had won three series against Australia. In 1953, England sneaked home by winning the only decided game at the Oval, but the margin of victory in Australia two years later, had been three to one. The *annus mirabilis* of Jim Laker, 1956, had brought the Aussies to England, only to see them go home tail between their legs, thoroughly whipped to the tune of two Tests to one.

To all intents and purposes the English bowling strength was as good, if not better, than that of the side which had done so well in Australia four years previously. Indeed in many respects the fast-bowling assets of the sides were identical since Statham, Loader, Bailey, and myself had all made the long trip south on the previous tour. The addition of the fiery Tyke, Freddie Trueman – in the place of Alec Bedser – showed that on paper we were, if anything, stronger in the quick department. Since Tony Lock and Jim Laker replaced Wardle and Appleyard as the purveyors of the guileful stuff, it could hardly be put forward either that the slow-bowling staff was weaker.

Though the touring party was top-heavy by one, it was soon apparent that the inclusion of only two spinners had been a grave error. How we missed Johnny Wardle, and how soon we realised our mistake! In the early part of the tour and until John Mortimore of Gloucester was flown out as an additional spinner, we were continually forced to play three fast bowlers every match, so that either Tony Lock's game knee or Jim Laker's arthritic finger could be given a rest. Wardle's inclusion would have been invaluable, not so much through the value of his orthodox spinners, as by his great gift of being able to bowl the mystifying chinaman and the tantalising and elusive googly. I have it on the very good authority of Keith Andrew that Johnny's left-handed wrist spin is not easy to detect, but his main value to the M.C.C. would have been to make the ball bounce more than the ordinary run of slow bowlers. No wrist-spinner holds out very much hope of turning the ball sharply on the bone-hard Aussie wickets, but because they throw the ball up more they make it bounce more, and cause considerable difficulty to the batsmen who, like the normal run of English players, show a reluctance to leave the crease to meet the ball on the half-volley. Without exception, every side we met in Australia had a wrist-spinner. The New South Wales tweaker, Peter Philpott, had me caught off a long-hop which I tried to square-cut, to find that the ball had risen shoulder-high so that I dollied it into the hands of cover! The best leg-spinner on the M.C.C. side was – take a bow to Tom–Tom Graveney!

I regard the incident which led to the exclusion of Wardle from the touring side, after he had been originally chosen, as unsavoury, unnecessary, and one which showered a great deal of disrepute upon the heads of cricket. Mine is not to reason why Yorkshire dispensed with his services, for that issue is purely a domestic one, and should have been settled within the county of the broad acres, not before the whole country. But I find it hard that a man already chosen for a tour should be taken off the boat because of a parochial question, albeit a widely publicised one. There is not the slightest doubt in my mind that Johnny Wardle's reaction to his dismissal by Yorkshire, and the subsequent action of the M.C.C. in dropping him from the touring party, severely impaired the striking power of the team sent abroad. On the practical side of the question, I am amazed that Johnny rushed into newspaper print, to say things about Yorkshire cricket and its administrators which could easily have been said and written upon his return from Australia. Yorkshiremen are no fools, and I think many people will agree that the Yorkshire committee would have had to present a far more feasible argument than the excuse of team-building, to warrant the exclusion of their senior professional and a current international cricketer. If Wardle had, in the words and idiom of the North, 'said nowt', I think the Yorkshire Cricket Club Annual General Meeting of 1960 might have been, to use a euphemism, a little eventful. The moral is that he who first throws mud must expect a little to come off on himself.

Whatever the pros and cons of the Wardle argument, no doubt exists in my mind that his loss robbed the English attack of some of its penetrative power. In his place, and doing the work of two bowlers, was Tony Lock, a man of infinite capacity and many moods, and the possessor of the finest and puffiest game leg imaginable. The hard Australian wickets continually jarred and aggravated his knee to such an extent that he had to strap up his leg, virtually from the ankle to the thigh before he could bowl on it. Incomparable in attitude and bowling skill in England, 'Bo,' as we called him, had to give the Australian wickets best. His outlook towards the enemy batsman is remarkably aggressive for a slow bowler, and his fandango of suspense and frustration as the ball beats the bat are well-known sights on every cricket ground in England. The trouble in Australia is that it is far from easy for the orthodox slow-bowler to beat the bat by spin. The process of learning that it is impossible on such wickets to pitch on the leg-stump and knock down the off every ball can be a long and expensive one. Tony found this out to his cost.

When the side for Australia set sail from Tilbury one September afternoon in 1958, the thought crossed my mind that we were a well-balanced party, well-equipped for the job before us. Our inventory included seventeen players to take care of the cricket business, two managers to look after the office work, a physiotherapist to guard our physical welfare, George Duckworth to physically guard our luggage, and about forty Pressmen. What could be better balanced!

We were a racing certainty to be successful both socially and cricketwise. The Australian public still remembered Freddie Brown from his valiant tour of 1950, and the rotund figure of George Duckworth, and his characteristic stentorian appeal, were still clear in their minds even from the 'Bodyline Tour'. Even the Aussie players were pessimistic about their chances in the series, particularly after the M.C.C. beat the Australian eleven at Sydney. Neil Harvey thought that England would beat Australia right up to the first Test, and he had no reason to be of any other mind. The M.C.C. side was as strong, if not stronger, than it had ever been and Australia's team showed little difference and few changes from those we had beaten in the previous three series.

The 1958 trip was my second tour of Australia but my third visit to the continent. Only the previous year I had sailed to Australia and returned with a wife. During my short visit I was asked many times whom I thought would win the coming Test series, and every time I replied with confidence that the victors would be England, and gave the reasons why. It was true I had the opportunity to see O'Neill in action, and I was forced to admit that here was a talented player, and a potentially great cricketer. Even the speed of Gordon Rorke failed to shake my confidence in my country's cricket, for when I saw him bowl the first over at the Melbourne Cricket Ground in the game between Victoria and New South Wales, the total at the end of the eight balls was 19 for two. There were three boundary-wides, a four no-ball, various other sundries, several acrobatic saves by the wicket-keeper, – apparently selected because he was used to keeping to Gordon – and two dismissed batsmen who had had their stumps razed to the ground behind their backs. The margin between the England and Australian sides, I forecast, would be four Tests to nil, and even now, though I admit I picked the wrong side, I like to think that I was clever enough to nominate the correct score.

To the practised observer it was clear, even at the outset of the tour, that all was far from well within the English camp. There were several symptomatic disturbances which rippled and disturbed the stagnant English pond of complacency. The Wardle episode stirred up cricket's dung-heap, and while the stench was still strong in the nostrils, Jim Laker announced he was unwilling to go with the touring side. It later transpired, and was revealed in print, that Jim had disagreed with his Surrey and England captain, Peter May, and felt that he could not serve under him abroad while such a relationship existed between them. Boudoir and dressing-room revelations smack of sensationalism, and have been decried in many quarters as doing a great deal of harm to the good name of cricket. People of this opinion should put themselves in the position in which Jim found himself, and ask themselves how they would feel if their captain accused them of not trying on the field of play. I think that Jim had every right to clarify and justify his position and his reasons for refusing initially to go. The most criminal aspect of the whole situation was that a captain and one of his chief bowlers should eventually consent to go on tour together when such a poor relationship existed between them. A touring team that contained such a clash of personalities and conflicting interests had no chance of building up any *esprit de corps*. To me at any rate, it is now obvious that common sense should have told

Peter May he was not going to get the best out of Jim Laker.

It is easy and convenient to find excuses for the failure of the last M.C.C. side to Australia; indeed it was such a controversial voyage that excuses came too easily and too conveniently. It was so handy to be able to blame everything on the heinous crime of throwing, and to say quite simply that we were 'thrown out'. People who seek exculpation behind the skirts of the throwers or jerkers simply cannot face the hard facts. We were beaten by a better side. I should go further than saying we were beaten; we were thrashed, and should the spirit move any seekers after knowledge, the records will show that England, by going down 4-0 in the series, sustained the most decisive defeat ever inflicted on an English touring team in Australia. What I find incredible is that a side which, with few changes from the victorious sides of past years, embarked for the southern hemisphere with such high hopes, should have been beaten so soundly by a team which differed very little from those they had previously conquered. Everyone must admit that the respective margins of eight wickets in the first and second Tests, eight wickets, ten wickets, and nine wickets in the fourth and fifth, hardly leave any room for doubt as to the drubbing we took. What was the reason for this sudden and radical change in English cricket fortunes?

Certainly the Australians batted consistently better than their M.C.C. counterparts. McDonald and Burke always gave the down-under boys a sound if not brilliant foundation to their innings, whereas England depended upon the vagaries of Peter Richardson's form with the bat, and a permutation upon a succession of injured opening batsman. Milton broke his finger, and Willie Watson was delayed from hitting true form by the surgical removal of a foreign body from his knee-cap. It is amazing how the M.C.C. has been hit over the past few years by a succession of touring injuries which, although they seemed small at the time, have severely handicapped team selection. In South Africa Johnny Wardle injured his cartilege so badly that he had to have it removed. The irony of the injury was that it was caused by playing snooker!

The Aussies did more than open well. They batted in depth, and they followed up McDonald with players of such calibre as O'Neill, Harvey, Mackay, and Benaud. Wally Grout's number in the order was nine, yet such is his batting ability that he has opened on occasions for his state side, Queensland. I can assure you that at times the English bowlers were glad Ian Meckiff was playing, even though the batsmen were not. At least it gave us a crack at a tail-ender who had no aspirations or great ability with the bat.

In the final analysis, the players who took part in those Test Matches must admit that the Aussies batted better, fielded better, bowled better, and were captained better. Benaud, though new to the task of captaincy, proved that he was an old hand at the task of leading men. He generated a team spirit which made the Aussies a fighting unit, and it says volumes for his captaincy that veterans such as Harvey and Lindwall agreed to serve under him, although their experience might have given them a prior claim. Only once was captain Benaud forced on the defensive and only once did he set stereotyped, defensive fields to his bowlers; at Sydney, when his negative tactics produced a draw with a silver lining. It meant that it was impossible for Australia to lose the series. Captaincy is a peculiar privilege. It is an honour yet a burden, a pleasure yet a responsibility. However able the captain, he can only be as good as his team allows him to be. I feel that the English team practically gave Benaud a written guarantee that his term of office would be successful, for though I would agree that the better side won, I should never say that the disparity in playing ability was correctly represented by the margin of England's defeat. Potentially England were a far better side than their performances on the field led one to believe.

If I had to put my finger on any one point that contributed more than any other to our downfall, it would not be that we were the worse side, so much as that we were not a side at all. The tone of the whole tour was pitched on the keynote of discipline, and as far as I am concerned a pinch of team spirit is worth a lorryload of discipline. The policy the management was going to pursue was indicated as soon as the team set foot on board the ship, when we learned that although the Saturday evening social get-together was to continue, no spirits were to be drunk during the meeting. Nowadays the Saturday evening club has disappeared altogether, sacrificed on the altar of discipline. The great 'must' will never run a side as well as 'ought'. When I played in a Test Match, I went to bed early, not because I was ordered to do so, but because I felt that if I did not, I should be letting my team-mates down on the following day.

In Adelaide, minutes before the fourth Test was due to start, Jim Laker declared himself unfit, because his arthritic finger was troubling him and he felt that he would be unable to spin the ball. I have not the slightest doubt that Jim's finger was most painful. It certainly looked as though it hurt. But what struck me most forcibly about the whole incident was that at the moment when the side needed him most, when to lose the Test meant to lose the series, our team spirit was such that Jim did not feel the least inclined to risk playing and damn the consequences. I was not surprised, for the policy of the management had not been to foster loyalty, however unnecessary that should have been.

My foretaste of what was to follow came when we were a few days out of Tilbury. During dinner I chanced to call Peter May 'Peter', as I might well unconsciously do, since I had played cricket with Peter long before he became captain of England. After dinner Freddie Brown asked me to go on the boat-deck with him for a few words. When we were alone, he told me under no circumstances must I call Peter May by his first name again. In future it was to be 'Skipper' at all times. I am the first to admit that these instructions had been issued at the outset of the trip. We had even gone to the ridiculous extreme of inventing names for disciplinary purposes. The manager, Freddie Brown, was to be known as ''Ger' or 'Mr Manager', while Desmond Eagar was to be known as 'Cash' since he took charge of the financial side of the tour. I was under the impression that the official titles were to be used for official functions, and while we were on the field – the right times and places for discipline and formality. Furthermore Peter and I had mutual friends in Australia, and until I became used to the saddle of Peter's formal name, it was a source of embarrassment to me while christian names were being bandied around. The ties of discipline and respect are tricky knots with which to fumble. Sometimes they strengthen the bonds between captain and team; too often they merely open a gap between the leader and his followers.

For Peter, the player, I have nothing but admiration. I have never seen his peer in his time. More than any other batsman I have met, he possesses a terrific power of concentration and application. Outwardly unassuming, modest and quiet, inwardly he is driven by a dynamic compelling force which drives him to get his head down and score runs. And after he has scored a hundred he forces himself to concentrate and scores another century. His cricket is full of self-determination, concentration, strength, and runs – and what better recipe is there for success. After all, did not Don Bradman say that cricket was 90 per cent concentration and 10 per cent ability?

I think that Peter May's tragedy as a captain lies in his inability to convey this driving, compelling force within him to anyone else. More than any other skipper I have ever played under, Peter lacked the common touch. Freddie Brown, when he played as a captain on the field, wielded the arbitrary power to which his position entitled him; but off the field he was approachable, he liked his pint of beer as well as the next man, and it did not matter if that person had been the object of his anger on the field. Every man is entitled to be aloof and pursue his own way, but this policy in a cricket captain, particularly off the field, can be disastrous.

As a tactical skipper, Peter was criticised unjustly for his decision to send the Aussies in first after having won the toss in the fourth Test at Adelaide. It is easy to condemn after the gamble has been taken and failed, but put yourself in Peter's position on that fateful morning. Australia were leading in the series with two wins and one drawn game. England needed to win both the remaining matches to draw the rubber. An indecisive game would have been of no use at all. Therefore it fell to England's lot to bowl out Australia twice and to force an issue; whether a draw or a loss it did not matter. With such facts at his fingertips, the English captain had to take the offensive. He failed in his gamble, but posterity will not know how close he came to success! In Australia's first innings mammoth total of 476, Colin McDonald contributed 170. Yet the first ball he received from Statham passed over his middle-stump by a whisker! It was another of 'if only'. What would have happened if McDonald had gone in Brian's first over? Cricket records might have shown a different result for the series.

There were moments on the tour when I felt that not only was there a rift between management and the ordinary rank-and-file, but also that there was little sympathy between amateurs and professionals. It is natural that there should be a schism in a community of men of widely differing educations and tastes, and that a Cambridge graduate should enjoy pursuits far removed from the ken of an ex-miner. The segregation of a touring side into amateur and professional is only a nominal distinction nowadays, but since most amateurs earn money from cricket it is silly to emphasize even a distinction in name only, when team spirit is at stake. It does little to improve the morale of a touring team when it is known that the amateurs may even receive more money in expenses than the professional earns in salary, when tax has been deducted.

Quite often the enigma of the amateur baffles me. As a captain, he is supposed to be the superior of the professional, since he does not depend upon the game for a living. Should he be reliant upon cricket for his daily bread, he would, like a professional skipper, be accountable to his employers for any action he took on the field of play. Captaincy under such restraints is supposed to lack the imagination which independence gives to the amateur.

Here lies the great lie of amateurism, or should I say shamateurism: scarcely an amateur in the country can truthfully call himself financially independent of the game and its ramifications. Show me a boss who will employ an amateur cricketer, allow him six months holiday with pay during the summer, and I will show you a very rare man. Most of the non-professional players still depend upon cricket for a living, if not directly, at least indirectly. Several find their way into the ranks of county secretaries or assistant-secretaries and many more receive royalties from books, autographed cricket bats and other sporting equipment. Unless they are endowed with strong moral principles, their names appear at the head of some newspaper article at one or other stage of their careers. There are indoor cricket schools to be exploited, and probably at the end of an amateur career the security of a job reached through cricketing connections. Can players who exploit such opportunities and openings honestly say that they do not earn their livelihood from the game? I once met a very frank, front-line amateur who confessed that he was making so much money as an unpaid player that he could not afford to turn professional! A person who earns his living doing something he loves is a very lucky person, and I was always proud to admit that I was a pro. If I were asked to define an amateur, I should say that he was a cricketer, shrewd at heart, who from ultraistic sooner than altruistic motives, is ashamed or unwilling to admit that he earns his coppers from the game. In the final count, he still makes his living out of the game.

I am not lambasting amateur cricket in principle, for I think the financial tangle of present-day cricket could be solved by the unpaid player and reduced overheads. It is also my contention and belief that the less the player's financial dependence on a professional game, which ends at forty, the greater his individual overall security. True amateur cricket has something to contribute towards making the game more of a spectacle. If it can make cricket less a matter of unemployment or a job, less a question of life or death, win or lose, then it can bring back entertainment value to the game and make it a more light-hearted affair. In principle amateurism is an admirable conception. In practice it can be completely otherwise, and if amateur cricket means the continued tolerance of a privileged group within the game, then I say 'No' to it with my whole heart.

When I returned from Australia after my private visit of 1957 I discovered that an official apologia had been issued on behalf of amateurism, and that the main argument for the continuation of the state of grace was that amateurism was one of the few bonds that remained with tradition. It is all very well for amateurism to hide behind the skirts of tradition, but I was always taught that the best traditions incorporate the qualities of the past with the advantages of the present. Tradition is a tricky commodity to traffic in, for only too often a custom handed down from the past can be linked with the nasty word privilege. Once privilege is mentioned in the same breath with amateurism then the very word stinks in the nostrils.

I am the first to grant that an amateur needs genuine ability to succeed in present-day cricket. If he is chosen to play for England there can be no doubt that he is as good as and better than most of his professional brethren. But there is always the nagging thought at the back of my mind that, admitted they are good, and the distinction of the amateur is only superficial, yet they are viewed more favourably than the pros by the powers that be. Many of the amateurs have gone to the same public-schools as the selectors; if they had not the same alma mater, then perhaps they attended the same university. I know I always view my old school-mates with favour, and I feel that, in proportion, it would be true to say the same about the rest of the world, no matter what their position. I would not throw my brother out of the window to prove that a perfect stranger means as much to me, and neither would, I dare hazard, the England cricket selectors. Consequently I was not too amazed when Peter Richardson, after a very poor Australian season, and the loss of a whole cricket season, was still asked if he was available for the West Indies trip of 1960.

Human nature is such that the preference of cricket selectors for the amateur is a natural predilection, but in spite of any allowances for inborn prejudices, privilege within the framework of cricket remains morally wrong. I know this amateur-professional apartheid does nothing but harm to any team and particularly to a touring side.

It only makes team spirit all the more difficult to maintain. The pretended and superficial classification into paid and unpaid players ought not to exist in the man-to-man relationship of cricket.

The success of any M.C.C. side abroad depends as much upon the players' ability to get on together and live in the same hotel, as it does upon their cricketing skill. Though I have been an offender in the very fault I condemn, this is one of the reasons why I am opposed to taking wives on tour. Seven months away from home is a long time, and it is natural that husband and wife should wish to be together; but in spite of these considerations, it is obviously true that wives on tour monopolise their husbands and separate them from the boys more than is good for the team. I have often thought that if permission were granted for every wife to accompany her husband on tour and, if they were in a financial position to afford it, the M.C.C. would very shortly find themselves in the position of having to appoint a manageress as well as a manager for the touring party. It is also true that the presence of a few privileged wives on tour could easily cause resentment in the ranks of those who were neither lucky nor rich enough to bring their better halves with them.

Management of an England side is often beset by many perils; press relations, speeches at public functions, team morale, illnesses which spring from worry, and on one remarkable occasion an allergy to alka-seltzer! Of the management of the 1958 trip, I think it would be kinder to say that it took two people all their time to do a job which Geoffrey Howard had done far better by himself during the previous visit to Australia.

Cricket kingdoms may come and cricketers may go, but what will remain for ever of the last tour to Australia will be the important questions: did the Aussies throw, and if so, did the throwers win the series?

I want to make my position quite clear at the outset. I was under no shadow of doubt that both Meckiff and Rorke threw in 1958. Their run-ups were mere apologies, and they just ambled to the wicket before pitching the ball at the batsman as fast as they could. For those who labour under the misapprehension that it is easy to throw the ball whilst on the move, just let me advise them to try it. To stand at the wicket and pitch is comparatively simple; but to throw on the run means the ball can fly in any direction. I know because I tried it in the nets at Sydney, and the result was terrifying both in its speed and its bodily threat to the batsman, who worked on the theory that if I did not know where the ball was going, then he certainly did not. When one consciously throws it is easier to hit the ground harder, and so I found it was far easier to bowl the bouncer with a bent arm than it was in the more orthodox and accepted style.

At no time during that disastrous trip was I deluded into thinking that it was the throwers who beat England. There are people who will disagree with me on this point. I only add that even if they are correct in their assumption that it was the throwers who contributed largely to our downfall, then it was largely our own fault. Meckiff came under our inspection very early in the day; we were all of the opinion that he threw. Godfrey Evans, indeed, wanted to take positive action on the issue, and see that the Victorian bowler did not have the opportunity of making his pitch at us. Dynamic management and the desire not to antagonise the host country let sleeping throwers lie and Meckiff bowled us out in the second innings of the Melbourne Test.

If we inspect the bowling figures for the Test Matches, the part played by the chuckers in the rubber will soon become obvious. Between them, Meckiff and Rorke played in six Tests altogether, and during those games they took twenty-five wickets, an average of 4·1 per game. Davidson and Benaud played in every Test Match, a total of ten Tests between the two, and in the course of those games they captured more than twice the number of wickets taken by the so-called chuckers – fifty-five. This makes the average of the straight arm bowlers, five-and-a-half wickets per Test Match. Figures are not everything and yet they can give us a very good indication of the relative importance of this much inflated question of throwing in Australia.

Chuckers are not a new breed of men. William Denyson tells us of Nyren and Lillywhite, who because they bowled round-arm and with the hand raised above the shoulder were saddled with the odium of being throwers. Lillywhite it is said, raised his hand so high that it could be seen above the fence which surrounded the cricket ground. All this took place in the 1830s and '40s; more than a hundred years ago. In more recent times it is rumoured that the South African 'Buster' Nupen and the Aussie Ironmonger did not visit this country because their actions were so suspect that their Boards of Control deemed it unwise to send them.

Wherein lies the cunning and the strength of the thrower? Though I am willing to contend that Rorke and Meckiff were hot decisive factors in the Tests of 1958 and '59 I will admit that they did cause two of our best batsmen a great deal of trouble. Perhaps more than anyone else, it was Colin Cowdrey and Peter May who were puzzled by the chuckers. Significantly enough, Peter and Colin were the two best natural timers of the ball in the side, and so it was obvious that the people who bent the arm for the wrong reason, had the knack of making the batsman mistime the ball.

The danger man among the suspect action bowlers is not the person who throws every delivery, but rather who only throws or jerks the odd one. In this context I am reminded of the batsman who, batting with Jack Hobbs, was very worried about the kinky action of one of the opposing bowlers. Between the overs he approached the great batsman at the other end with these words:

'Eh, Jack, the fellow at this end is throwing.'

'Aye,' said Jack. 'Don't say anything. They might take him off.'

There is no magic in the word 'throw'. I do not think for one minute that to throw necessarily means to project the ball any quicker. It may seem to the batsman that the ball arrives faster than he expects it, but this is not because the ball is in itself faster, but rather because the bowler's action is curtailed by the throw or jerk, and the ball leaves his hand quicker than was anticipated. Normally a batsman judges the pace on any ball by the speed of the run-up, the violence of the body action, and the power and swiftness of the full swing of the bowler's arm. Imagine how the batsman is caught napping when the bowler who has been delivering with a perfectly straight arm suddenly whips in a throw. The striker is slow on his stroke because he is waiting for the full swing of a ramrod straight arm and instead he receives the curtailed jerking action that, with its shorter arc, catches him with his bat still poised in the air. It seems to be two yards quicker than the other balls, but its additional pace is not from its speed through the air; it is derived from the quicker and shorter arm action. The thrower is a most deceptive bowler to face. Since he has no need of a fast approach, which will only make him more erratic, he merely lopes up to the wicket, and complacency grows in the batsman every second. If he has never faced a chucker before, he might well be excused for thinking: here's another of those medium-pace bowlers masquerading under the name of 'fast'. Even the swing of the arm, slow at first, seems to bear out his thoughts. Then suddenly the bowler's arm straightens convulsively and the batsman is left high-and-dry, waiting for the ball which he confidently expected to be half as fast. Many a mournful clatter in the timber-yard has been the result of this complacency.

At first I thought it would be possible to become used to the new vogue in bowling. After all it should not have been too difficult to accustom oneself to the shorter swing of the arm and the corresponding suddenness of pace. It might mean that the future Test players might be loath to lift their bats too high and that stroke play and brighter cricket might die a little quicker than they are doing at the moment. The thrower, by the very sudden spasm of his action, would find it almost impossible to swing the ball to any degree, and his threat would lie only in his peculiarity of pace. What a multitude of sins is covered by those three words: peculiarity of pace. Much later I realised that the chucker can, with no change of his action, throw either very fast or very slow. The arm position remains the same, and the bowler, if we can call him that, merely keeps his wrist behind the ball and throws a really quick one down, or he undercuts the ball and delivers a hanging, slower ball. Without exception, all the batsmen who have played against the jerkers or throwers have said the main trouble lies not in the speed of the bowling, but in the difficulty of the striker in picking up the flight of the ball and knowing whether it is a real thunderbolt, or an innocuous slower one.

More often than not it is the good players, those who lift their bat high before making their shots, who are troubled by the chuckers. I know that Peter May and Colin Cowdrey were both embarrassed by Meckiff and Rorke, not because of the undoubted speed, but rather because their technique of batting had been perfected over years of practice by playing against bowlers who used the full swing of the arm. Under such contrasting conditions it was natural that their timing should have been astray.

Most of the argument about what is a throw and what is not a throw I condemn as so much hot air. It is a pity that the people who sit around worrying about how to define a throw have nothing better to do. The demand for a clearer definition of the suspect or condemned action merely indicates to me not that the umpires are in some doubt as to what constitutes a throw, but rather that they have not the courage of their convictions. Many years ago a certain Mr Knight said in the print of a London magazine, about another throwing controversy, that when a horse breaks into a canter, there is no need to define what a canter is, it is enough to witness it. He added that the same might be said about throwing. I entirely agree with him. I have actually fielded while a suspicious-looking bowler has been performing, and I have heard the square-leg umpire say:

'I know he throws, but I am not going to no-ball him. I did it last time, and look what happened.'

The problem of throwing lies not in the definition of the fault, but in the application of Rule 26 and the backing the umpires, as a professional body, would receive from the law makers and administrators if they enforced it strictly.

There can be no toleration of the throwers, for in common with many mortal diseases, throwing can be contagious. When we first landed in West Australia we met a certain bowler by the name of Slater. 'Spud' Slater bowled slow off-spinners not by inclination, but by compulsion, since the umpires in grade cricket had no-balled him when he tried to throw his quicker stuff. The paradox of the whole situation was that although Slater was not allowed to bowl fast at the grade cricketers he was permitted to hurl them down at the M.C.C. His four scalps against us included that of Peter May, genuinely beaten by what can only be euphemistically termed an unexpected turn of speed. So it was that the touring management cast the team in the role of Aunt Sally, and we had to sit back and take the knocks. The South Australian side contained two fast bowlers by the names of Tretheway and Hitchcox. Such was the undoubted nature of their bowling action that we had no hesitation in dubbing them, 'Tre throw ey' and 'P itchcox.' In Melbourne the redoubtable Ian 'Chuckiff' awaited us, and Gordon Rorke was our daily medicine when we played New South Wales in Sydney. Only in Brisbane were there no throwers in the Queensland side, and this was largely attributed to the the staunch opposition to the 'jerkers' of Ray Lindwall, the state captain. Ray told me that he is going to write one last book, as a memorial to a dying art, and in true Fenimore Cooper tradition, he is going to call it: 'The last of the Straight-arms.'

It is a sufficient commentary on the infectious quality of throwing that, looking around the international sides of the world, including the England side, it would have been possible over the last few years to have nominated a dozen bowlers whose arms seemed to be bent at the moment of delivery. Rorke and Meckiff are not the sole culprits, though ill-proportioned publicity may make them seem to be so. What of Tony Lock, and Peter Loader's bouncer? They, just as much as the Griffins, Chester Watsons, and Gilchrists of this world, are, unlike Caesar's wife, not above suspicion. It is important when we tackle this question of throwing that our own camp is in complete apple-pie order. The first country officially to raise the problem of throwing in open committee must expect to be the cynosure of critical eyes. How sincerely and how thoroughly are we attacking the enemy within our gates? I dare to say not very conscientiously. Time may heal everything, but it cannot hide the fact from my eyes that we are afraid of the chucking question. The umpires are afraid in general to take an open stand against the blatant thrower, and the legislating authorities are afraid to lay down clear rules for interpretation, or to back up the umpires in any one definite firm course of action. The question of drag raised its brutal and controversial head over twelve years ago, and can anyone today say that we are much nearer to a solution? There is still a wide variation between umpire and umpire as to how much the fast bowler is allowed to drag, and no one has the guts to make a stand on the question. I dare say we shall be in the same position with regard to throwing in ten years' time.

My eyes were first opened to the extent to which players imitate the throwers, when I visited the West Indies with Jim Swanton's side in 1955, As there were only thirteen members of the side and two of these were quickly injured, it was thought wiser to employ some of the local talent to bowl at the batsmen in the nets. They were not fully-fledged cricketers in the true sense of the word; they were just the young boys who stood around the nets and watched. One of them, dressed in ragged short trousers, no shoes, and a gaily coloured shirt, continually bowled out Hubert Doggart with the most prodigious off-spinners, delivered with a very bent elbow. Hubert, who is a schoolmaster, left the net after a very uncomfortable ten minutes, and walking up to the boy congratulated him on bowling so well.

'Well bowled, lad,' he said, and then added in his magisterial manner; 'there is only one thing. I think that when you bowl, you manage to turn them on these pitches because you throw.'

The boy looked up at Hubert, all red gums and white teeth and said: 'That's alright, boss. Massa Lock does it and Massa Johnson does it. I sure can do it.'

Make no mistake, we have such boys in this country. Sometimes they even permeate as far as county cricket and too often we have a tendency to ignore their transgressions because they are not in the Test Match sphere.

Until we pay as much attention to the fault in the younger generation as we do in the Test Match players, we are not tackling the problem of throwing conscientiously. Until we remove the mote from our own eye we are not in any position to be the authors of legislation against throwing in other countries.

CHAPTER TWELVE

# Some Unhappy Decisions

Many people are of the opinion that the ogres of the last tour of Australia and the true architects of England's defeat were Meckiff and Rorke. It is a totally disproportionate view. It would be equally true to say that the Australian pitches were the main reason for our downfall, for in a minor way they did undoubtedly contribute towards it. Before the team ever sailed from home, it was obvious to all that the selectors had put their faith in an extremely strong battery of fast bowlers. To put it bluntly, the Aussies saw us coming. They were not going to be caught on wickets which suited our bowlers. They had suffered that experience at Manchester in 1956, when Jim Laker took nineteen wickets in the match. It was however a source of great amazement to me to find that the wickets which had suited fast bowling so well in the previous visit had now been tamed and reduced to the pace of an English pitch. Even the Perth and Sydney wickets which had been bone-hard, pace-packed, and green when it rained, were now on a par with the feather-bed strips one normally associated with the Adelaide Oval. In 1954, I had taken ten wickets in the Sydney Test Match. Four years later, Freddie Trueman was carrying to the wicket-keeper standing back on the second bounce! The W.A.C.A. cricket pitches at Perth used to be rolled so much that the playing area was three inches below the level of the rest of the square. Now they are brown instead of green, and their present pace, compared to their former speed, is like a middle-aged amble by the side of a youthful sprint. How had the metamorphosis happened?

Most Australian squares are made of Bulli or Murray Creek soil; a clay mixture that, when baked by the Australian sun, produces a hard, true, and pacy wicket. It is a versatile surface, too, for it is normal to see a football match being played in ankle-deep mud over an area that six weeks later is to produce a Test Match wicket. Its failing as a cricket-pitch is that it has a tendency to crack when subjected to too hot and too constant a sun, and to counteract this shortcoming the recognised practice is to plant the playing area with couch-grass. This type of coarse grass, though it undoubtedly succeeds as a binder of wickets, also has one bad quality: its dense root growth not only knits the pitch, it forms a cushion of grass which also takes the pace out of the wicket. When the M.C.C. visited Australian shores in 1954, quite a few curators had taken the couch-grass out of their pitches in an attempt to quicken them up, little dreaming that England would produce a fast bowling combination to hoist the Australian 'quickies' on their own petard. They produced doubly disastrous results, for not only did England and her fast bowlers sweep all before them, but the wickets showed a regrettable tendency to crumble on the third day. This was especially true of the Melbourne Oval. However, by the time my second tour came along this deficiency had been remedied, and the couch was once more safely planted. England, of course, still expected every Australian wicket to be a fast bowler's paradise, and consequently packed the touring party with five pace bowlers – a policy that had paid dividends on the last occasion. They were cruelly deceived, and the touring team often found themselves playing with three seamers and one spinner on wickets whose pace and bounce would have been equally at home at Northampton. I can put it no lower. From the outset, we were handicapped by an original selection that, in the light of the slow wickets, can only be described as top-heavy, and consequently our bowling effective was halved.

Umpires were also a variable quantity compared to the previous tour. For many years Mel McInnes had personified to my eyes all that an umpire should be. He was firm, just, deliberate, unobtrusive, and knowledgeable. At least such had been my judgment on the last tour, and I continually sang his praises to my companions who had not seen him in action. We were in for a cruel disillusionment. From the outset his conduct was calculated to make the hairs on every 'Pommy' back bristle. Rubbing the ball on the ground to remove the shine and so enable the spinners to gain a firmer grip is normal practice in this country. Tony Lock often briskly brushed the ball against Mother Earth before turning at the end of his run and coming in to bowl. Mel McInnes stopped him and told him that he was not to use the ball so roughly.

'Why the so-and-so not?' asked Tony.

'You will rub the ball out of shape,' came the incredible reply.

Tony's look was eloquently expressive.

I do not mean to imply for one minute that the umpires cheated or were unjustly biased against the English team.

The main problem which faces Australian umpires is that they cannot gain enough experience from the limited opportunities they have of practising their mysteries. Very few first-class Aussie players ever feel the urge upon retirement to take up the white coat. Perhaps it is because they have better things to do, or maybe they feel, quite rightly, that an umpire too often is more sinned against than sinning. Assuming that most Aussie arbiters have no great cricket experience, it means that their first-class experience is limited to three or four games per season. As the travelling distances are so great in Australia, the state umpires only stand in their own province's home games: a practice which seems at times to be almost too convenient. Apart from these limited opportunities, the umpires are confined to gaining their experience from the week-end grade cricket. To draw a parallel in this country, though I have the greatest respect for our own league umpires, I suggest that it would be unfair to expect them to stand in a Test Match. Yet such is the case in Australia. In the circumstances it is unnatural to expect their umpiring to reach an exceptionally high standard, for I do believe the art of judging a cricket match is one of the many things in this world that does require a great deal of practice.

While the controversy was raging on the subject of Australian umpires, one English critic was heard to propound the theory I have just expressed on the Aussies' lack of first-class umpiring experience. Rumour has it that Sir Donald Bradman overheard the remark and broke into the conversation to exclaim:

'That's all nonsense. Mel McInnes played several times for South Australia before his eyes went.'

Then of course he realised what he had said.

The occurrences and the umpiring errors of the Adelaide Test were the most amazing cricketing *faux-pas* I have ever witnessed. I shall never forget them. The day was hot, and my first turn with the ball came about an hour after Australia had been put in to bat. As I began my spell, Australia had made a good start and were almost 50 for no wicket. The half-century had just been hoisted and lunch was a few overs away, when, feeling frustration and anger mounting in me, I managed to dig a fast one in and bounce the ball shoulder-high at Jimmy Burke. He only managed to parry at it with his bat and brushed it in passing with his glove. Almost all the pace had gone from the ball, and it speedily dropped towards the turf. It seemed that the ball could not possibly carry to Godfrey Evans until that remarkable man, flinging himself forward, just scraped a glove underneath to grasp and hold the ball before it bounced. To appeal was almost unnecessary, but as Burke made no move to go, the umpire's verdict was called for. On the radio, Keith Miller was telling the world at large that Burke was out. The broadcasting-box was behind the wickets and there was no doubt in the minds of the people in that vantage-point that Burke was out, caught behind the wicket. They had seen the ball deflect off his gloves and Evans make good the catch. To my amazement Mel McInnes gave Burke not out. I was so furious that it completely spoiled my lunch.

It fell to my lot also to be involved in what must have been the most remarkable run-out incident in modern Test cricket. Colin McDonald, batting with consummate ease on a placid pitch, had accumulated almost 150 runs;

during the latter part of this massive total he had been assisted by a runner, because of a torn thigh muscle. It was a mystery to me why Peter May had to be so polite as to allow a man with so many runs to his credit to bat with a runner, particularly when the runner was Jimmy Burke, his normal opening partner, a person well used to co-operating with McDonald. Colin hit a ball hard into the covers, and forgetting that he had a runner at square-leg, immediately and instinctively made as if to hobble down the wicket for a single. Brian Statham swooped on the ball in the short extra-cover position and returned hard to the bowler's end. I gathered the ball and broke the wicket with Burke still two yards out of his ground. Mel McInnes, seeing the instinctive reaction of McDonald, had hurled himself to one side of the wicket to be ready to make a snap run-out decision. Unfortunately he chose the wrong side of the wicket and had his back to the side of the pitch where McDonald's runner, Burke, was scraping to make good his ground. As I took off the bails, I remember looking up into Mel's face. He looked at the broken wicket and then glanced down the length of the pitch to where Colin McDonald was still in his ground at the other end. There was a smile playing on his lips and I could almost read the thoughts as they sped through his head:

'At last, here's a decision there won't be any quibble and argument about.'

For a few weeks he had been subjected to a continuous barrage of criticism from the English Press and a constant demand that he should be replaced on the umpire's panel. Here at last was a straightforward, honest-to-goodness, open-and-shut case of a run-out, with no necessity to consult the photo-finish camera. His finger went up almost immediately and I, the bowler, heard him say quite clearly: 'That's out.'

Suddenly he realised what had happened and a look, not of horror but of resignation, took the place of his former happiness. As he had not seen the actual run-out, he had no alternative but to reverse his decision. So it was that in the space of thirty seconds he gave McDonald both out and not-out. When the second phrase, 'not-out', passed his lips, pandemonium and confusion broke out on the field, and I, at the bowler's wicket, was in the midst of it. Peter May rushed up to the wicket from cover and asked: 'Is he out or not-out?' McDonald himself strolled up the pitch to ask the same question, and then went to ask Jimmy Burke's opinion of the incident. Jimmy wanted to stay at the wicket, and I am afraid that when McDonald backed up his opinion, tempers became a little frayed and a few hard words were uttered. Bouncers became the order of the day, and with McDonald now throwing his bat at every ball, the tempo of the game became positively exhilarating. Finally, twenty runs later, Colin McDonald was bowled by Freddie Trueman having a terrific yahoo. The incident faded, and the cricket assumed its sedate Test Match pace once more.

I could not but feel sorry for poor Mel. Throughout the whole disturbance he had hardly said a word apart from the two most telling phrases of the whole incident. His umpiring had come a long way in the wrong direction since 1954. In those days I should have rated him as second to none in the world. Four years later he was the centre of controversy, penalising Freddie Trueman for his drag, Tony Lock for rubbing the ball in the dirt, and even going to the extreme of publishing a series of articles in the newspapers to justify his decisions. In my own mind I am sure he realised he had made some bad decisions.

As I look back on this stormy interlude, I find it hard to realise that Mel McInnes is not a villain of the blackest dye, but a tall, quiet-spoken, studious, bespectacled person and the most amiable individual in the world. In spite of my criticisms of his conduct of Test Matches, I like to think of him as a friend, who was harassed and heckled into making mistakes not in keeping with an umpire of his standing. I shall always remember him as I last saw him, outside the Melbourne dressing-room during the fifth Test Match.

'You know, Frank,' he said to me, 'this is my most enjoyable Test Match.'

He was not standing in the game!

Like Mel McInnes, I am of the opinion this was a tour to be forgotten, or at least to be veiled by the discreet curtain of the past. It was gall in my mouth to have Peter May hand me the ball, with defeat by ten wickets staring us in the face in the fifth Test Match, and to hear the words: 'Bowl until they pass our total, Frank.'

'Damn it,' I thought. 'This is a far cry from Melbourne in 1955. I can still show them though!'

So it was that I tried to recapture the rhythm, speed, and exhilaration of former years: to feel the familiar stiffening of the knees and the gathering of the shoulders for the last titanic effort to hurl hatred with the ball at the batsman.

The score-board only records the fall of one Australian

wicket in their second innings of that match. The entry in the book reads:

'J. Burke, lbw, bowled Tyson.'

'Tis not so great as Sydney, or famous as Melbourne in 1955, but 'tis enough, 'twill serve.

CHAPTER THIRTEEN

# Goodbye to the Razor-edge

No one can take away the enjoyment I have drawn from cricket. It has given me many happy moments of companionship, thrills, and satisfaction, but I have always been fully aware that professional cricket, in the proper perspective of the practical business of living, is only a phase and not a complete way of life. When I was twenty-four and about to take the plunge into the paid game, I made myself two promises. I was going to play first-class cricket only as long as it was enjoyable and not when it was sheer hard, physical work and no fun; and I would withdraw from six-day-a-week cricket while it was still not too late to take up another job. Do not mistake my motives or sentiments. I should like to play cricket for a living until the day I die. Unfortunately I have not been able to find a county cricket club willing to pay my salary after I cease to be an effective force in their side. Every young professional would do well to remember that county cricket clubs are not charitable institutions. Though a will-of-the-wisp benefit may ever lure them on with promises of security there comes a time when age calls quits and the hard business of beginning another job from the bottom comes at the age of forty. Even if you are a well-known cricketer it would hardly be fair to expect to step into an unaccustomed profession at executive level. The best time to quit professional cricket is while there is still time to take up an alternative career that will provide employment up to normal retirement age. I like to think I have hung on as long as I could possibly afford to do so.

Since cricket has afforded me so much pleasure, it grieves me to leave the game when the immediate outlook is so gloomy for its future. Every cricketer in the country will say that grounds all over the country, though they have improved in their appointments, still lack one very important requisite – spectators. At times it has almost embarrassed me to play professional cricket before a vast concourse of fifty people, especially when I think that they had to pay to come in. The brutal truth about cricket is that many county cricket clubs' coffers have a hollow, empty ring, and in many parts of the country the game is slowly becoming insolvent. One county cricket club secretary confided to me, and I shall keep his confidence by withholding his name, that at the end of the season, after all expenses had been paid and all the clubs' securities had been sold, there was exactly £28 in the kitty.

I am not a dismal Johnny, nor is it my intention to write a jeremiad of cricket. There is no doubt in my mind that professional cricket will continue for a few years to come. People tell me that county cricket has never been solvent, and that before the war many shires were in the county championship entirely because of the support and the odd thousand pounds of various patrons. Nowadays of course the world has changed around us and there are no longer people who can afford or, for that matter, want to give a thousand pounds to support the county game. Instead of the patronage of the few, we have the support of the many, expressed every week by the support they give to the football pools run by cricket clubs.

There is a strong vein of irony running through cricket, a summer game followed by winter crowds. When the vast web of the supporters' club pools was but an idea in the minds of a few money-spinners, the stronger clubs of the championship, with large memberships and loyal followings, saw no necessity for such financial schemes. The Yorkshires, Lancashires, Middlesexes, and Surreys of the table were the last to be affected drastically by the falling-off of attendances. Only the Leicesters, Northamptonshires, and Warwickshires felt the pinch early and laid the foundations of what are now thriving financial organisations. Too late the goliaths of the cricket world saw the red danger-signal up the line and the red ink on the bank balance. By then competition was too strong in the field of football pools and many of their efforts flopped dismally. Now it is very probable that the weakest shall be the richest, and the strongest shall be the poorest. It would almost be cricketing poetic justice if in a few years' time, due to financial stresses and strains, only the weakest cricketing counties were left in the county championship.

I have no doubt that professional cricket will be played in England as long as there are supporters' football pools to subsidise and keep it; but from a player's point of view, it is an unrewarding experience to play in empty grounds. Worse still when I played, I knew that many of the game's financial foundations were rotten, and while I enjoyed making my living from cricket, I often felt that I was walking the razor-edge of security, living on a bankrupt business. If I may put a question to the reader; how would you like to depend for a livelihood upon a business which you knew to be making an operational loss of thousands of pounds a year? What would be your answer? I dare hazard a guess that you would be looking for another position.

The complacency in some cricketing financial circles is truly amazing. Quite often the Colberts of cricket are prepared to rest on the achievements and the profits of football pools, without giving a second thought to whether cricket as a paying entertainment concern is a success or not. Apparently it does not matter whether people come to watch cricket or not, provided the privileged few who can afford to take time off to watch mid-week cricket can ride their favourite hobby-horse and run the game. Too often this attitude is reflected in the professional player, who feels no necessity to entertain the public but is content to justify his place in the side by virtue of an annual thousand runs and a hundred wickets.

But as I say, it grieves me to leave the game just now. Every time I pack my cricket bag and leave a ground it gives me a twinge of regret to say good-bye to yet another happy game of cricket. Last season gave me many such moments of sorrow for I realised that when I said farewell to the first-class cricket grounds of this country, I might never see many of them again.

Cricket has provided me with many happy and eventful hours, and I am grateful for the sublime experiences which have come my way. I have played on beautiful grounds all over the world. My feet have trod the ecclesiastic calm of the Adelaide Oval and I have lifted up my eyes to its hills, whose claustrophobic closeness gives the whole city, its cricket ground and its people, an air of intimacy and friendliness. My sweat has watered the unproductive plains of South Africa's Newlands, and my mind has been constantly delighted by the blue-bearded Table Mountain with its crisp, white table-cloth of cloud. It is easy to come off the field weary and tired in body on such grounds but the mind is continually refreshed, surprised, and delighted by the beauty all around.

There have been less pleasant experiences on the field of play. I have sweltered in the tropical heat of several countries. Trinidad's Queens Park has overwhelmed me with its Turkish bath air, its giant Coca-Cola signs and the predatory green fronds of waving palms against the background of the island's mountains. I have breathed in the airy fire of Durban's heat, melted in Melbourne and broiled in Brisbane. In Ceylon the humidity was such that to breath was like gulping whole mouthfuls of damp cotton wool, while the coloured crowd hung from every palm tree, pole and perch, whistling, moaning and hissing like a pitful of snakes. I have laughed with the Aussies, drank with the Springboks, and moaned with the English. What more could a man want?

Cricket has taken me everywhere and shown me places that otherwise I should never have been able to visit. I have caught tunny-fish in South Africa weighing 140 lb. I have fished New Zealand's Metaura river, risen to fish Lake Taupo at four in the morning – and I have trapped more fish in the morning than batsmen in the Tests. In Australia, I have slung my hook for sharks in Sydney Harbour, and three times hauled up the anchor, thinking I had caught a monster. The game has shown me wonderful things. I have seen the glow-worms in New Zealand's Waitomo Caves, her hot springs and geysers at Rotorua;

Bombay's Brabourne Stadium, already an oven at five in the morning, and I have driven there through the waking streets where millions of people sleep every night on the pavement. Magnificent liners have carried me through the Suez canal and its surrounding aridity. I have bathed on Hawaii's Waikiki beach and surfed in Barbados. In San Francisco I have seen Alcatraz, the Golden Gate, had a Turkish bath in a golf-club and, a few short hours later, in New York, visited a musical show and spent the night on the town in Greenwich village. Tom Graveney and I discovered that breakfast in Bermuda can cost £3. I have seen cricket played on the campus of Princeton University. Cricket has taken me twice round the world and revealed to me the wonders of travel. The names of the places I have visited sound remote now: Singapore, Bangkok, Puerto Rico, Calcutta, Fiji, Madras, Nairobi, Bahrein, Calcutta, Khartoum, and even Wake Island. The game has broken down social barriers for me. I have mixed with millionaires, Princes, and even, once talked about cricket to the Princeton class of '21.

But cricket is more than a social register and a conducted tour to me. It is a whole host of wonderful people, great players and loyal friends. As a defensive bat there was none to rival the incomparable Sir Leonard. He had probably forgotten more about the technique of batting than I shall ever know. His image springs readily to mind, his bat seemingly glued to his left pad, his eyes ever watchful, his body leaning into the stroke, shifting and moulding his shot to accommodate the spin and swing of the ball – an ikon of concentration, revered by generations of English cricket-lovers. What a kaleidoscope of impressions a mere eight years of Test cricket have left with me! The fluid aggression of a Harvey hook; the unpredictability of Compton's mood and his great eye for a ball; the guts of Edrich, the doggedness of McGlew, the smooth, bulkless timing of Cowdrey, and the ferocity of May at the wicket.

There have been great moments too: the personal thrill of wrecking the Australian innings at Sydney by taking ten wickets, and of sweeping all before me in the second innings at Melbourne on the Glorious Fifth of January. But looming way above all these wonderful moments is the sheer thrill of bowling fast.

If I had my life to live over again, I would not ask for success alone, sweet though it is. I should only want to be allowed to bowl fast once more. To those who have bowled quick, really quick, there is no comparable feeling in the world. The sudden clutch of suppressed anticipation as you mark out your run: the hesitancy that blossoms into arrogant confidence as, from a shuffling slow start, the stride quickens, lengthens, and becomes smoother; two yards from the wicket now and time to give it everything you've got; the body swivels, left hand plucking at the clouds, right arm swinging in a deadly, ever-quickening arc as the batsman appears in the sights over the left shoulder; the left leg is raised high, ready for the final plunge and the body is poised and ready; crash! – the skull shakes and the muscles of the body jar screamingly, as the front foot thumps down like a pneumatic-hammer and the ball rockets on its way at the cringing batsman, pursued as if by an avenging angel, by the bowler's flying body. What power there is in bowling fast! What a sensation of omnipotence, and how great the gulf between this sublime sensation and ordinary, mundane everyday existence!

I began with a quotation, I end with a misquote, when I say that, from fast bowling I have discovered to the full:

*'How good is man's life, the mere fast-bowling.*
*'How fit to enjoy, all the heart and the soul,*
*'And the senses for ever in joy.'*